The Man on the Bench.

*An amazing story of a homeless schizophrenic
who taught a community to care*

h. Alton Jones

54 Candles Publishing
San Diego, California

54 Candles Publishing Company
2726 Shelter Island Drive, Suite 47, San Diego, CA 92106

www.54Candles.org

ISBN 978-0-9845545-0-8

To the ladies in my life – Liz, Tempest and Mom

A civilized society is one which tolerates eccentricity to the point of doubtful sanity.

Robert Frost

Table of Contents

Introduction

There are events in the lives of all human beings that transcend explanation. Life is an ongoing lottery where a seemingly insignificant chance meeting on any given day can change the course of a person's life, a community, a nation and even the course of humanity.

So it was in 2003 when I first met Jeffrey Pastorino. It was an event that altered the course of my life. I later learned this homeless, mentally ill man unknowingly touched the lives of many others who chanced to see him. He impacted an entire community and helped it redefine itself. In as much as the members of that community are part and parcel of the greater community of California, the nation and the human race, it can be argued this man helped steer the ship called *Humanity*. The magnitude of his contribution is debatable and only with the passage of time can it be better defined. The wings of a butterfly floating above the flower covered hills of central China imperceptibly alter the wind currents in their wake. Through a series of cause and effect relationships, they may ultimately trigger a hurricane in the Gulf of Mexico. So too may the actions of this humble man yield momentous changes in the course of history. What will be the consequence of some future random act of kindness born of the relationship with Jeff Pastorino?

The first time I saw Jeff, it was obvious he had his share of problems and challenges. I knew little about the plight of the homeless in America and less about mental illness. This book is not a scholarly dissertation on those subjects. Although I have since done a reasonable amount of research in the preparation of this book, I readily yield the floor to those more qualified.

You will discover many mysteries remain when telling the story of Jeffrey Pastorino. Despite interviews with family, friends and acquaintances, some parts of the story are subject to a small amount of "creative interpretation". I have made every reasonable effort to be as accurate and true to the facts as possible. But with HIPPA laws currently extant in this country, medical records, if still in existence, remain sealed. Certain facts were reconstructed from Jeff's own writings and statements; others have come from family members and witnesses. Given the limits of the records available, this story is as accurate and close to the whole truth as possible.

This work could not have come to fruition without the valuable and caring help of many people. No one has contributed more than my wife Liz McCarty. Arguably, she is a co-author. She helped with much of the research and over the years became a friend of "The Mayor". Her insights and suggestions weighed heavily as the friendship developed and as the book was being written.

Jeff's brother, Chris, has been a wonderful and generous contributor to the effort. He dealt with countless traumatic situations throughout the past year and stood up to pressures few could carry alone. He acted with total honor and decency and is himself someone to be revered and respected. His contributions to this book have been invaluable.

My thanks also go out to my creative and talented copy editors, Marcie Rothman and Victoria McCarty. Sam Warren of Bookwarren Publishing Services helped with valuable input and suggestions. Without Pete Miller, this book would undoubtedly remain little more than a pipe dream. He was a one man public relations firm. Ann Campbell's efforts have been spectacular. Her heart tilled the garden in which so much human kindness has grown. Her tears watered and nourished that garden until it blossomed in its full glory.

I'm also grateful to have known that very special person named Jeffrey Q. Pastorino and for the things I've learned from him. After all, it was through him I came to realize we all spend at least some of our time sitting on the bench.

Chapter One
Point Loma, California

The weather in Point Loma, California is close to perfect today. I know this because the weather in Point Loma is close to perfect every day. It is one of a half dozen places in the world with a Mediterranean climate. No place in the forty-eight has it better.

Point Loma is a quiet village, a vibrant community, an active social venue, a seedy tenderloin, an exclusive refuge for the reclusive, a natural wonder, a sailor's Mecca, a big city, a little town. Its people are rich. Its people are poor. They are successful, failed, young, old. They come from entrenched, blue-blooded California families, mega-yachts and military bases. They are fishermen, tarot card readers, beggars, boat workers, bankers and bakers. They include cops, prostitutes, politicians and topless dancers. Beauty queens live there. Singing idols are their neighbors. They are the down-and-out, the up-and-coming and the too tired to play. They are Anglo, Korean, Mexican, European, East Indian, and American Indian. They are white, black, brown and yellow. They are uniquely American in their diversity. Point Loma is a test tube in the laboratory of the American experience. It is the echo of yesterday and the promise of tomorrow. There is no other place on the planet like Point Loma.

The village of Point Loma lies within the city of San Diego. It rests on a rocky peninsula jutting southward into the Pacific Ocean. It is that peninsula that protects the idyllic waters of the great natural harbor known as San Diego Bay. When the massive Navy ships stationed in San Diego enter the harbor, their bows point toward the heart of the village. Sailors see great patches of brightly colored bougainvillea cascading down the steep hillsides of the point. Red crowned parrots screech at dawn and dusk. The village is ninety miles south of Los Angeles and ten miles from the Mexican border. It is a small town within the big city.

It was on Point Loma that Juan Cabrillo, the first European to ever set foot in what would become California, landed on September 28, 1542. In was in Point Loma that Richard Henry Dana spent much of his time before writing about his adventures in *Two Years Before the Mast* nearly two hundred years ago. It was from a dirt airstrip named "Dutch Flats" in Point Loma that Charles Lindbergh first flew his "Spirit of St. Louis", a plane designed and built by Ryan Aeronautical Company. The Ryans remain one of the prominent families in Point Loma to this day.

Around the dawn of the twentieth century, Portuguese fishermen looking to take advantage of the bountiful tuna schools off the coast of southern California began flocking to the village of Point Loma. Saint Agnes Catholic Church still conducts services in Portuguese. Since 1910, streets in the village have been closed between the church and the Portuguese Hall for the annual *Festa do Espirito Santo* with its parades, dances and feasts. It is not uncommon to hear Portuguese spoken when walking in the village. Some residents still call it "Tunaville", a nickname earned when tuna fishing was one of its major industries.

A section of Point Loma known as La Playa served as the original port for San Diego when it was founded in 1769. Rosecrans, the main street running through the village, was originally La Playa Trail connecting the fledgling city to its port.

The north end of Rosecrans flows into a bustling, commercial area with a somewhat seedy character. Adult bookstores form the backdrop for the homeless people holding up their brown cardboard signs reading, "Homeless veteran, need help, God bless" or "Why lie? I need a beer." Traffic on Rosecrans is heavy with thousands of commuters passing to and from a handful of major military installations located on the peninsula.

The character of Point Loma gradually changes as you head south on Rosecrans. A mile past the "World Famous Body Shop", just around the corner from Larry Flynt's Hustler Club, the road narrows to four lanes as it comes to Liberty Station, an historic Navy training area reborn as a planned residential community. Tens of thousands of American sailors trained for battle in World War II at "NTC San Diego". Clark Gable, John Wayne, Dean Martin and Jerry Lewis, Abbott & Costello and countless other stars brought patriotism to the silver screen with movies filmed at Liberty Station. Despite its rebirth as a twenty-first century community, Liberty Station retains much of the architecture of its glorious past as a major military training ground. On the hillside above Liberty Station, the homes grow bigger as you continue south.

After another mile, you're in the village itself. Old and new buildings come together to create the neighborhood of Roseville. The streets are lined with hundreds of magnificently beautiful jacaranda trees. Their abundant lavender blossoms overwhelm the senses and give the village a purple hue during the summer months. In the shade of the jacarandas, fallen flowers make a popping sound like plastic bubbles under the feet of the locals, mariners and tourists walking in shorts and shirtsleeves. The spirit of the village is defined by the many neighborhood restaurants, boat yards, sailing supply companies, and marine related businesses. Adjoining Roseville is Shelter Island. More than three thousand pleasure boats and yachts call the dozen or so marinas home.

Cross Talbot Street and you've suddenly left Roseville and entered "La Playa". Although a few of the old fishermen's humble homes remain, La Playa is dominated by luxurious mansions ranging from magnificent on the low end to indescribable on the high end. A million dollars may be an adequate down payment on some of the estates in La Playa; for others, it will take a bit more. Many of the homes on La Playa's hillside have spectacular views of the unique city skyline of downtown San Diego, the San Diego Bay and the open ocean to the south and west. The lights of Tijuana, Mexico are visible to the southeast and when the ocean mist is cooperating, the Coronado Islands off the coast of Mexico are clearly visible to the south.

The residents of La Playa include rock stars, professional athletes, giants of the fashion industry, writers, media icons and stalwarts of business and industry. It is one of the most expensive areas of San Diego for a reason. With a near perfect climate, breath-taking views and its unique character, La Playa is just up the road from paradise.

It was into this unique village that Jeff Pastorino walked one summer day in 1992. He sat down on a bench at the corner of Rosecrans and Avenida de Portugal in the heart of Roseville in the village of Point Loma. He sat there until he died in 2009. This is his story.

Chapter Two
Homeless in America

More than a million Americans will try to sleep without the comfort of a bed tonight. Some will lay on cardboard sheltered from the elements in the covered entrance of a retail shop near Union Square in San Francisco, their tattered jackets their only protection from the cold night air. Others will hang their heads as they slump on a park bench along Michigan Avenue in Chicago. Someone in San Diego will wedge himself into a corner of a bus stop bench long after the last bus has left the streets for the night. Others seek warmth in bushes or small groves of trees. Glassy eyed acquaintances huddle together in the darkness of the alley behind the liquor store and split a bottle of cheap wine.

Public perceptions of the homeless in America are tainted by the observations of a seemingly endless array of "bums" working the intersections in major cities. Often they're days or weeks removed from a bath and they repulse most of those who pass them by. A few sympathetic souls wish them well.

"Homeless veteran – hungry – anything will help. God Bless," reads the sign written with black marker on brown cardboard. "Will work for food," says another placard. From time-to-time, you stumble on a grinning corner barker holding a sign proclaiming, "Why lie – I just need a beer." It seems to work; cars occasionally roll down their windows and hand him a few coins or a dollar bill. I've even seen a kindred spirit hand a beer out the car window to a smiling beggar.

To the regular commuter, it looks as if the homeless have a system whereby street corners or intersections are allocated on some semi-formal basis. Once a corner is "assigned", the same person appears to have the rights to it until some twist of fate, like illness, death or relocation, causes him to disappear. Like chattel, it seems to be passed on to the next eligible beggar. I can't help but wonder if the organization of some street people is such that each lucrative corner isn't franchised by a higher ranking homeless person for a percentage of the take.

Free enterprise surely applies to those at the bottom of the socio-economic ladder just as it does at the top. I once sat down next to a particularly articulate beggar in a covered bus shelter in San Diego and struck up a conversation. He looked to be nearing his fortieth birthday with a dark, full beard. He seemed well educated and was more than frank when he told me his story. He admitted he had a serious problem with alcohol abuse. He worked the intersection when he'd nearly sobered up and needed money to buy more liquor. As I listened to his story, I couldn't help but realize that with a bath and a change of clothes, he could have easily found a job that paid him well. Then he told me he would work the corner for perhaps an hour. A typical hour's work brought him about forty dollars. True, he had more charisma and was a better performer than most, but the "paycheck" for his job was better than most.

Who, when confronted with the image of a homeless, placard wielding beggar, doesn't wonder what has brought him to that condition in life? Why doesn't he just get a job? He must be a drunk or drug addict that can't escape the habit. Sadly, many times, that is the reality. But if only it were that simple.

There have been attempts to characterize and quantify the homeless population. Simplistically speaking, approximately half the homeless have serious problems with substance abuse, alcohol, drugs or both. The substance abuse strains family and social relationships that might otherwise be the source of support and assistance in getting back on their feet.

Roughly a quarter of them are homeless because they lost their jobs, homes and possessions. During hard economic times, this number rises dramatically. In this group, I include victims of domestic violence, natural disasters, or other unexpected emergencies such as major medical problems that may have led to financial disaster. It is also the members of this group that stand the best chance of getting back on their feet.

The remaining quarter of the homeless population is on the streets because of significant, often untreated, mental illness. It is this group that accounts for most of the "chronically homeless". The mental illness makes it next to impossible to obtain employment. Depending upon the nature of the mental illness, social relationships may be out of reach. The victims of the illness may have virtually no hope of breaking free from the conditions that make them homeless.

Homelessness in America has steadily increased since the 1960s when state mental institutions began trending toward a community based treatment approach. In the late nineteenth and early years of the twentieth century, states scrambled to build facilities to house the growing numbers of mentally ill. But in 1963, Congress passed the *Community Mental Health Centers Act*. As a result, many long-term psychiatric patients were turned out from state mental hospitals. State budgets for mental health care and treatment were cut. Facilities such as the Northville State Mental Hospital in Michigan closed.

The community based treatment concept, as well intended as it may have been, let many mentally ill patients slip through the cracks in the system. They ended up on the streets. The social and political dynamics of the late sixties and seventies during the Vietnam War exacerbated the problem of homelessness. For some of the more free spirited people of the times, living on the fringes of homelessness became the vogue. Life in Haight-Ashbury, Greenwich Village and innumerable communes almost glorified a lifestyle only one step removed from the transient existence of the homeless. Politics and social conditions set the stage for an explosion of homelessness.

The problem gradually worsened throughout the late seventies and into the early eighties. During the Reagan administration funding for American cities was drastically reduced. Funding for affordable housing assistance and community based mental health treatment and follow-up all but disappeared.

In the early eighties, the economy went into a tailspin. Unemployment rose to nearly eleven percent. Foreclosures ballooned. People lost their jobs, their homes and their futures. Homelessness in American went through the roof, a roof the victims didn't have.

By the late eighties, the magnitude of the problem was becoming overwhelming. The McKinney-Vento Homeless Assistance Act was signed into law in 1987. It helped create soup kitchens, shelters and other vehicles intended to help the homeless. Although it mitigated some of the suffering of the homeless, it did little to address the root causes of the problem.

The problem persisted and an increasing number of Americans learned how to turn their backs on these unfortunates. For some, it became a matter of routine to envision all the homeless as villainous bums too lazy to work. The corner beggar was there because his character flaws and weakness for alcohol or drugs brought him his just reward. He was a bum because he deserved to be a bum. He earned his position in life. He was there because of the choices he made, not because of anything within the control of the person stopped at the light with the windows of his Mercedes rolled up tight. A contemptuous glance toward the bum and blessedly the light turned green.

Some community leaders and politicians tried to face the problem. Numerous councils were convened to study and deal with the epidemic of homelessness. Despite the tireless efforts of many, the problem continued to grow. Some attempts to deal with the issue were not the most compassionate. Law enforcement agencies made sweeps of an area to run out the homeless. If nothing else, they forced them into the blighted areas. If they couldn't solve the problem, maybe they could at least contain it.

It was interesting to observe that the homeless population of Pacific Beach, California had included the same faces for years in the early nineties. Before the 1996 Republican National Convention in San Diego, police made a sweep of the area and one day many of the familiar faces of mentally ill homeless people disappeared. They never returned.

Municipalities passed laws prohibiting "camping" or sleeping, eating, begging or even sitting in public places. Arrests were made. Fines were levied. The brute force method obviously did nothing to combat the causes of homelessness and was doomed to failure. In 2006 after a series of legal challenges, the 9th District Court ruled that "making it a crime to be homeless by charging them with a crime is in violation of the 8th and 14th Amendments" of the U.S. Constitution. Criminalization of homelessness wasn't the solution to the problem. It was folly to think that a night in "the tank" would somehow bring a mentally ill person to his senses and prompt him to get a job as a stockbroker. The causes of the problem needed to be identified and dealt with if hope was to blossom.

Chapter Three
California Dreaming

I wondered if we were going to survive the storm. It had been nearly three days since it began and it was still snowing continuously. Every ninety minutes like clockwork, we were hit with an avalanche. We could hear it coming for a couple seconds before it actually hit us and buried our tents below six feet of snow. We had just enough time to quickly roll over and get on hands and knees, using our backs to try and keep the tent from collapsing completely and suffocating us. Once the avalanche ended, we would begin the process of digging out of our tent, clearing as much snow as possible and repairing the damage. If we moved fast enough, we could finish in time to get back into the tent and try to rest before the next rupture of the snow pack above us.

In 2003, I was part of a mountain climbing expedition tackling one of the more challenging routes to the 20,321 foot summit of Mount McKinley or Denali as most climbers refer to it. Like all of us, a mountain has its moods. Denali is no exception. In fact, when Denali is in a bad mood, it can be one of the world's most brutal mountains and inhospitable hostesses. For some reason, she seemed to be really pissed off for much of the month we'd spent climbing her. I had climbed four of the world's coveted "Seven Summits" within the past two years. I had been considerably higher, but I'd never met a mountain as mean as Denali.

As a boy growing up in Michigan, I played ice hockey on the frozen ponds of winter. I was familiar with temperatures of thirty-five degrees below zero. Wind chill temperatures on Denali had approached one hundred degrees below zero. I'm not sure I can describe what it's like to be that cold. One of our fellow climbers could no doubt do greater justice to the task; he lost eight fingers to frost bite on the climb. When it gets that cold, virtually every one of your actions revolves around staying warm.

We had been climbing for nearly three weeks and were approaching the 17,000 foot elevation when the storm hit. We surveyed our surroundings and dealt with our desperate need for shelter. We found it at the bergshrund, a gaping crevasse formed at the highest point of a glacier where it tears itself away from the mountain. We cleared an area just big enough to erect our four tents tightly nestled together at the edge of the "shrund". A cornice of snow and ice had formed on the other side of the crevasse. It curled over the crevasse about eight feet above it. It gave us some protection from the wind,

The author descending Mount McKinley

but more importantly, it caused the great masses of the recurring avalanches to pass over our heads and down the mountain. The six or so feet of snow that kept burying our tents was the slough from the avalanche. No one survives the direct onslaught of the massive avalanches that occur on the face of Denali.

With our tents teasing the edge of the bergshrund, a misstep could mean a fall into the bowels of the mountain. Some of the crevasses on Denali are estimated to be as deep as four thousand feet. If someone fell in without being "tied in" with a rope, the chances of surviving were close to zero. The only question is would the person die before coming to rest or would he come to a stop, a crumbled bundle of human bones and succumb to hypothermia quickly thereafter. We remained intensely aware of the schrund and made every effort to avoid its depths.

Despite the existence of the monstrous crack in the mountain, we set each of our tents such that the exit faced the schrund. This was because about two feet past the other end of our tents, the mountain dropped off precipitously for more than two thousand feet. In situations like that, gravity is not your friend. A fall in that direction would have assuredly been fatal. The area where the body would have ultimately come to rest was striped with hundreds of crevasses. There was a good chance the lifeless body would have been swallowed up by the mountain. Admittedly, when the weather ultimately cooperated, the view from our perch was breathtakingly magnificent. Even staring into the depths of the bergshrund was spectacular with its ice walls of surreal greens and blues. But the fact remained; one step too far in either direction and life was over. The body wouldn't have been found for a minimum of a thousand years until it was extruded into the melting snow at the bottom of the glacier.

We had three long days to contemplate our flirtations with mortality. It was near the summer solstice so we had no nights whatsoever. The only thing that kept the sun from shining on us constantly was the dense blinding snow provided courtesy of one of Denali's meanest blizzards. The joy of experiencing an avalanche every ninety minutes added to our sense of humility.

When the storm finally abated somewhat, we were pinned in our makeshift campsite for another day. We had to locate climbing gear that had been buried. We discovered some of our support gear had been washed away by the uproar of the mountain. We had to evaluate snow conditions with test pits that helped us estimate the chances of continued avalanche. After nearly four days, we finally continued our ascent.

Something else happened during the time spent in our small and precarious perch near the top of Alaska. I'd had a revelation of sorts. It wasn't of a religious or particularly spiritual nature. It was closer to one of those "duh" moments we all have from time to time.

In the two years leading up to the Denali climb, I had spent months high on mountains in North and South America, Africa, Europe, Russia, and Asia. My wife of nearly a quarter century was always supportive, yet always apprehensive when I would leave for a major climb. She knew I'd had my close calls and that I'd not only seen the face of death, but touched it as well. Yet she quietly suffered the worry of not knowing when or if I'd come down from the heights.

Thanks to climbing, Liz also has seen much of the world. A typical itinerary was that I would fly alone into whatever country was home to the mountain d'jour. About a week before I was due to descend, Liz would fly into the city closest to the mountain. We'd then spend the next couple weeks seeing the host country. As nice as these trips would be, the truth remained that the climb itself was a very selfish act on my part.

The quest to conquer the world's big mountains is driven by many things. Alpinists see the beauty of the world from an angle few ever dream of. The spectacle of nature is singularly magnificent from the heights of the great mountains. Climbers also learn more about themselves as human beings than otherwise possible. They test their ultimate limits. They get to see the face of the little voice in the mind that drives all people to succeed or fail in life's toughest pursuits. Those like George Mallory who say they climb the mountain because it's there are trivializing. There are countless motives for spending weeks in nature's most ruthless conditions where the air is thin and the skin turns black, but all of them are selfish. No one climbs Everest for anyone other than himself.

Such was my personal revelation. As I laid in my tent on Denali bracing for the next avalanche and hours stretched into days, I felt selfish. My wife was home wondering if I was alive, periodically checking news reports for word of climbing disasters. She was with me on Mt. Hood when nine men fell into a crevasse. Three died and a helicopter crashed during the rescue attempt. The image haunted her every night during the weeks I was gone.

I thought about how finite our time is on the planet. I thought about how my time on the mountain was time away from the woman I loved and to whom I had committed my life. I felt selfish. I vowed to spend no more lengthy periods of time away from her. My next climb would start where there was a warm breeze, a sandy beach and Liz would be with me. Denali would be my last major climb.

As was the case with previous climbs, Liz arrived in Anchorage, Alaska about a week before my anticipated arrival. She rented a car and picked me up in Talkeetna. We enjoyed a week seeing Alaska. We talked about the future. When we boarded the plane bound for Phoenix, I left much of my climbing gear behind. We set our sights on the horizon and walked away from the mountain.

For years, whenever we had a chance to take a break from our business pursuits, we'd take the day long drive from the White Mountains of Arizona where we lived to Pacific Beach in San Diego. We had stayed in one particular hotel right on the beach so often, they had actually created a special rate class for us. We loved San Diego. The ocean, the cosmopolitan atmosphere, the climate, the diversity, San Diego seemed to be heaven on earth.

When Liz's father decided to keep his yacht in San Diego for six months out of the year, we were delighted. Well over a hundred feet long, it had six bedrooms and plenty of room for guests. When we returned from Denali, we headed directly to our suite on the sea. For three weeks, we would sit on the bow of the boat and watch the sun disappear into the Pacific. We watched as sailboats silently glided in front of us heading for their slips. They seemed so peaceful, so serene. With a soft, warm breeze, they were everything an avalanche ravaged tent high on the face of an arctic mountain was not. They also had plenty of room for both Liz and me.

One evening as Dennis Conner sailed by on *Stars & Stripes*, his America's Cup racing yacht, I gave Liz a furtive glance and said, "We ought to go take a look at one of those, not that I'd ever consider buying one."

I waited for her response. Assuredly, she would comment on such a ridiculous idea. The criticism never came. The next day, we were looking at sailboats. We told the salesman or perhaps in this case I should say sailsman, that we had no intention of buying. We just wanted to get an idea of what they looked like inside so that if we ever did think about buying one, we'd have an idea of what to look for in a boat.

The following day, we made our offer. We submitted a bid of $50,000 less than the asking price. We knew a reasonable seller would turn it down as an insult so we weren't really risking anything. It was a magnificent sailing yacht, a "blue water" boat designed and outfitted to sail around the world in the roughest conditions. It could generate its own electric power, make its own water, had room for three to four months worth of provisions. But we were confident the offer would be rejected.

The next morning, we walked from the marina on Shelter Island to a deli in the village of Point Loma. We enjoyed breakfast and a cup of coffee on the outside patio. Out of the corner of my eye, I saw someone walking. I looked up to see a disheveled man moving toward a bench on the corner. He carried a soiled duffle over one shoulder. I caught his eye and he quickly looked away walking a bit faster. He reached the bench, sat down with his back to us, lit a cigarette and stared into the distance. Probably one of the local nut-cases we thought. We'd been coming to San Diego long enough to know there was a significant problem with homelessness.

My cell phone rang. The yacht broker was calling. "Your offer has been accepted," he said. We were stunned. We were about to become yacht owners and at least for part of the time, San Diego residents. The man on the bench continued staring into the distance with complete indifference.

Chapter Four
Sail Away

We couldn't return to San Diego fast enough. We took possession of our new yacht and a beauty she was. The sailing vessel "Tempest" was a dream-come-true. As a now former mountain climber, no challenge seemed too great and it was a good thing. Neither Liz nor I had ever operated a fifty-foot sailboat.

Truth be known, I'd never commanded anything bigger than a "Sailfish", a glorified surfboard with a small sail and that was forty years before. Liz's C.V. was no more impressive than mine. Her only time at the helm of a sailboat was on a ten footer when she was in junior high school. A storm came up and neither she nor her sister, Victoria, could get the boat back to shore. Their father had to swim out and rescue the siblings who were fighting over how to get the craft home. We'd both been around power boats all our lives, but a twenty-seven ton sailboat with over a thousand square feet of sail area was a completely different animal.

We spent most of the next four months teaching ourselves how to manage the Tempest. Day trips ended with us backing the boat into our slip as the westerly winds tried to coax us broadside into adjacent ships, their owners braced for impact. My final act of each sailing day was to try and remain invisible as I scrubbed the black smudges that served as tattletales of our inexperience off the hull. I dreamed of the day I could bring the Tempest into her berth like a pro rather than arriving via ricochet, bouncing off the padded sides of the slip that was her home.

After four months of self-training, we actually reached a fairly high level of proficiency and I spent less and less time rubbing off smudges. With our self-imposed training regimen, we assigned ourselves one system or operation on which we would focus with each trip. The electric power system, the water-maker, anchoring, man-overboard drills, foul-weather sailing, each critical skill mastered in turn. We steadily moved forward in preparation for a lengthier trip into Mexican waters.

I was surprised to learn how much sailing and mountain climbing had in common. Rope skills, knots, weather prediction, hazard evaluation and team work are requisite skills in both pursuits. Good physical conditioning is also required to be safe and successful in both. It's not uncommon to see powerboat owners carrying a bit of a paunch, a cigarette and a can of beer, but sailboat operators are generally more physically fit, have a lower incidence of tobacco use and a greater propensity for a glass of heart-healthy red wine rather than a cold beer.

Although I'd sworn off mountain climbing, I had no intention of giving in to an unhealthy life style. Each and every day began (and still begins) with a brisk walk of four to five miles. A three mile run follows. When living on the Tempest, we would leave the marina at first light and walk the four mile loop that included the perimeter of Shelter Island, up Shelter Island Drive to Rosecrans and Talbot Streets where we would treat ourselves to a latte at Red's Coffee Shop.

On our first morning on the Tempest, we left at dawn. Our path took us past the intersection of Rosecrans and Shelter Island Drive. Union Bank of California has a branch office located at the corner. The building is less than ten years old, well maintained, nicely landscaped and a pleasant addition to the neighborhood. Half way down the block toward Avenida de Portugal the bank building gives way to its parking lot. Like the bank itself, it is clean, attractively landscaped and as parking lots go, pleasant to the eye. As we approached the intersection, we came upon a small plaza, perhaps ten by twenty feet situated at the corner. At first glance, we thought it might be a bus stop. It had three decorative metal benches. It wasn't a bus stop. A brass plaque thanked Union Bank for dedicating the small "community plaza" to the people of Point Loma.

Two of the three benches were empty. On the third, in the gray of morning, I could see the outline of a man sitting alone. His back was to us. He was smoking a cigarette. Next to him sat a red canvas bag. As we got closer, he continued to look off into the distance. He wore a hooded coat similar to the kind worn by mountain climbers. Hiking boots protected his feet. He wore the jacket hood up over his head as if he were cold or trying to protect himself from a rain that wasn't falling. I wore shorts and a tee-shirt. It was the same man we had seen as we had breakfast at the deli on the far side of the parking lot.

The following morning and each morning for the next couple of weeks we walked past the same corner. As it was on the first day, the man was sitting on the bench. He wore the same hooded coat. He was smoking a cigarette. And he kept his back to us never making eye contact. With each passing day, my curiosity grew, gnawing at my mind. I worked my way into position to catch a furtive glance of his face. He was clean shaven, but his clothes were soiled. His complexion was that of a man that spent much of his time outside in the elements, his face deeply tanned, his skin weathered. His hair was thinning and gray. He was somewhat overweight. He never acknowledged our existence.

Over the many years Liz and I have walked in the morning we have talked about almost everything imaginable. We've solved all of the world's problems, some two and three times. We observed human behavior and drew valuable conclusions about human nature. We conducted countless surveys. Do you know that 91% of the cars traveling along Rosecrans at 7:00 am toward the Navy submarine base every morning have only one occupant? Car pooling must be discouraged by the Navy.

We would sometimes pass a homeless person and wonder what unfortunate sequence of events led that person to his sad post in life. We talked about how it might be an interesting project to collect the stories of these homeless people, write a pamphlet with their histories and let them sell them on street corners. We thought they might make a lot more money selling their mini-biographies than by scribbling "Homeless vet, need help, God bless" on a piece of cardboard.

The hour or so we spent walking each morning involved discussions about politics, history, science, boating, climbing, cooking, taxes, health, family, strangers, global warming, Borrego sheep, the neighbors, the in-laws, outlaws and the previous night's dreams. Now a new subject crept into our discussion and in no time, began to dominate it. Who is that man? What is he doing sitting in the same place, wearing the same clothes, doing the same thing day after day after day?

As time went by, we had occasion to go into the village during the day to get parts and equipment for the Tempest. One day around the noon hour, we detoured past the corner with the plaza. There he sat, hood up, smoking a cigarette and looking away from the crowds driving along Rosecrans.

The Tempest was a more than comfortable habitation. In non-nautical terms, she had three bedrooms, two baths, a living room, dining room and office. Liz prepared dinner on the boat for the first few nights of our lives as sailors. But if Point Loma was to become our home away from home, it was time to get to know our new community better. We experimented with some of the many restaurants Point Loma had to offer. Our primary residence remained a small town high in the mountains of Arizona. We were delighted and overwhelmed to have such a great selection of dining choices.

We decided to give it a go at a quaint little bistro named *Luna Notte*. It seemed to have lots of charm, an interesting menu and a view of "the bench" a block away. We arrived as the sun disappeared into the Pacific. There sat the man on the bench smoking a cigarette.

Forty-five minutes later, it was dark and we were finishing our main course. We watched as the man stood up, looked around, put the strap of his bag over his shoulder and crossed the street. For the next ten minutes, he stood smoking a cigarette and scanning his surroundings. We ordered a dessert to share between the two of us. When we looked up, the man was gone.

"What do you know about the man on the bench?" we asked Rob Scott, the restaurant owner, as he scribbled our order.

"What man?" he retorted. It seemed the man on the bench was as invisible to the restaurant owner as we were to the man on the bench.

When he realized who we were talking about, Rob said, "Oh that guy. I don't know. He's just some crazy guy that always sits there. He's been there forever. We've been open for eight years and he was there when we opened."

"What's his name?"

"I have no idea," said Rob, "He's alright. He never bothers anyone. He just sits there."

That was like pouring gasoline on the fire that burned across our curiosity. The man had been sitting there for years. As we returned to the boat we couldn't help but talk and wonder about what must be going through the mind of a person that can quietly sit in the same spot for years. Hell, I couldn't sit still for thirty minutes without getting up and walking around.

The following morning we walked early. The man was sitting on the bench. He was there the following day and the day after that. He was always there. Just some crazy guy that always sits there. He was there from before sunrise until well after sunset. Same jacket, same boots, same pants, constantly smoking. And he was invisible.

As time went on, our credentials as sailors were becoming increasingly legitimized. We were gradually becoming one with the Tempest. We had sailed her to Ensenada, Mexico without any major incidents. It was no longer necessary to spend time rubbing black marks from the hull after docking. We felt like a couple of old salts and we started talking about taking a lengthy trip, maybe southern Mexico and Central America, maybe through "the canal" and into the Caribbean, maybe even around the world. We faced a few obstacles. In theory, we were still running two viable Arizona based companies. Liz was the broker and owner of a real estate company with three offices and nearly fifty employees. I was president and owner of a software development company with offices in Arizona, Florida and Australia.

We sat outside over coffee at the deli, the same one from which we first spotted the man on the bench a few months prior. We discussed what obstacles we faced if we were to sail away for a year or two. We concluded the software company could be managed remotely. If we outfitted the Tempest with high speed internet service and worldwide telephone access, I could continue to develop software, communicate with employees and keep the company on an even keel even if anchored in a quiet lagoon in the South Pacific. Other issues were easily resolved with internet banking, a mail forwarding service and other simple solutions. Our list of obstacles was reduced to only two items:

> *Sell the real estate company.*
> *Kill the cat.*

We weren't really thinking of killing the cat. We were just being a bit hyperbolic in a humorous sort of way. The cat belonged to our daughter for fourteen years while she was growing up. When she left home, she was kind enough to stick us with her cat when college housing prohibited pets. If we were forced to admit it, we liked the cat and considered her a part of the family, but she was the most useless animal I've ever known. She was deathly afraid of mice, too lazy to cast a shadow, didn't know how to play like a cat and was moody and sulky. She would not and could not join us on a trans-oceanic voyage.

With the man sitting on the bench in our rearview mirror, we left for Arizona to handle the sail away list. Liz made a call to a major real estate company in Phoenix thinking its owner might be interested in purchasing our business. Amazingly, an agreement was reached in a matter of minutes. The details had to be worked out, but the first item on the list was all but complete. It would take a couple of months to draft legal documents and make preparations for the announcements, but everything was moving forward.

A couple of weeks passed and we needed to get back to San Diego to outfit the boat with satellite receivers, world phone, internet and those technological tools and toys I'd need to run the software company. The evening before we left Arizona, the cat died – of natural causes. Cali was nearly seventeen years old. She was old as cats go, but given the way we'd phrased the second item on our list, we felt like we were getting a few incriminating stares from people that knew of our sailing plans.

It was close to the dinner hour when we arrived in Point Loma. We drove by the bench. There he sat, smoking a cigarette. It was a warm day with temperatures in the upper seventies. He wore his coat. The hood covered his head. Traffic was heavy on Rosecrans as hundreds of cars streamed out of the sub base a mile south of the village.

The next four weeks were full of deadlines on equipment installations for the Tempest. We had her "hauled" out of the water for fresh bottom paint and the installation of a massive copper ground plate necessary to shortwave radio reception while out to sea. Back in the slip, electricians mounted a bank of solar panels intended to give us an unlimited supply of electricity as we traveled the world. We had a massive battery bank installed. The diesel, known to sailors as the "iron sail", was torn down, serviced and rebuilt. The satellite dome was delivered and installed. We had our world phone and high speed internet service nearly everywhere in the world. The North Pole and a small area in Mongolia were excluded from coverage, but neither was on our sail plan. Sheets, lines and rigging were inspected and replaced if necessary. We provisioned the boat with three months worth of food. We stocked the library with plenty of reading material and filled a locker with DVD movies for entertainment. We even made certain we had our musical instruments on board, flute and piccolo for Liz and mandolin, guitar and violin for me. Everything was coming together better than we had expected. We were on course to set sail in six to eight weeks.

Our morning walks continued. We pondered the history of the man on the bench. We wondered what kind of mental illness would allow a human being to sit on the same bench day after day. To us, he was the source of constant wonderment. After leaving earlier than normal one morning, we found that the man would arrive around 6 am each morning. He would look around, pull a rag from his duffel and meticulously clean the bench before sitting down. As time went on, we learned this was his standard operating procedure, get there before sunrise, leave after sundown and stay on the bench for fourteen to fifteen hours every day.

In the weeks we spent preparing the boat for our world journey, we asked many of our new neighbors about the mysterious man on the bench. His story began to unfold. The most common version went along the following lines. He was highly educated, either an accountant or possibly even a C.P.A. He was a successful businessman and had been married. The details became a little sketchy, but it seems he came home and found his wife had been cheating on him. He cracked. He left his home and business and disappeared into the fog of a California morning. He'd been sitting in Point Loma ever since, a burned out, shattered piece of humanity, betrayed by fate and human nature, unable to recover from the trauma of his wounds. No one seemed to know if he'd had any children or what happened to the unfaithful wife who had so crushed his spirit. People just knew he was some crazy guy that had been sitting at the corner for as long as they could remember.

The Tempest was nearly ready to sail south. It was time to return to Arizona, finalize the sale of the real estate company, close up the house, say goodbye to family and friends, take care of a few last minute details and cast our fate to the trade winds. The morning we left Point Loma, we took an earlier than normal walk. It wasn't yet 6 am.

"The Mayor's not there," I said to Liz.

She looked confused, scanned her horizon and finally asked, "What are you talking about? The mayor?"

"Yes," I said. "The Mayor. The homeless guy that's always sitting on the bench."

"Why are you calling him the mayor?"

I explained, "He keeps regular hours. He reports to work every morning at the same time. He leaves his office every night at the same time. He's in his office every day, rain or shine, seven days a week. It just seems appropriate to proclaim him The Mayor of Point Loma."

From that point forward, our man on the bench became "The Mayor" of Point Loma. The Mayor was in his office when we drove off on what was intended to be our final trip to Arizona for one to two years.

Chapter Five
Some of My Best Friends is a Schizophrenic

The human mind is nature's most intriguing machine. I've left the formal study to the psychologists, neurobiologists and medical professionals. The mathematician in me suggests it is futile to try to understand the mind with itself as the looking glass. It seems this would lead to some type of a zero-divide error and my head would explode, sort of the philosophical analog to running faster and faster in smaller and smaller circles until you run up your own backside and disappear.

In recent years, I redirected the time I previously spent mountain climbing toward more diverse pursuits and areas of study. As an avid reader, I can't seem to get enough of history, philosophy, anthropology and other areas that reflect the machinations of the human mind and spirit. It's interesting to learn that so many of history's icons were more than a touch off life's center-line. Conversely, it seems that when studying history, very little is said about normal people. The curse of normalcy looks to be a condemnation to a life of boredom, not the type of life to which a mountain climber routinely aspires.

Normal people are not the ones leading us to higher levels of civilization. It is the deviant personality, the exceptional human being that breaks the boundaries of regularity and brings us kicking and screaming into the future. Rather than the bald eagle as a national symbol, we may have been better off with the loon or the cuckoo.

Life would be strange indeed if everyone was normal. There is great survival value to a culture as a whole to have individuals that can be characterized as odd-balls. Consider the fact that all high achievers are odd. If they were average achievers, they'd be... well, average. We desperately need our nutcases.

R. D. Laing, a famed research psychiatrist, philosopher and poet of the sixties and seventies argued the only sane people were those we declared as insane. After all, those afflicted with "madness" have built their own realities. In most cases, those realities differed dramatically from the realities we "normal" people share. The fundamental difference is that the artificial realities of the insane frequently work well. They don't have to follow the rules imposed on our worlds. They don't have to be logical. They have to follow neither man's laws nor nature's rules. They may look bizarre from our viewpoints, but they work quite well for the insane. On the other hand, our shared realities are sources of constant conflict. As proof, consider the invention of the middle finger. Laing raises an interesting question, "Who's really crazy, you or me?" I'm not sure I always have the right answer to that question.

When looking at the homeless people on America's streets, Laing's question occasionally comes to mind. Statistics indicate a quarter of them are chronically homeless because of serious mental illness. We look at them with their hand written cardboard signs and assume we're sane and they're crazy. We pass judgment while we sit waiting as a mechanical device displays a red light and exerts control over our lives; we're subordinate to the machine waiting for it to turn green and grant us permission to move forward with the mass of other drivers battling traffic. We're coming home from our jobs where we're at the beck and call of a capricious career ladder climbing boss who administers justice and guidance in our workplace. We go home, have a toddy to dull the pain, worry about the job, the taxes, the stock market, the mortgage and swine flu. We fret over our appearance, our social standing, the spouse, the kids, the car and the cash.

We look at the homeless guy when we're coming home rather than going to our jobs. That's because we have a "starting time" while the homeless guy sets his own hours. We worry about the mortgage, the taxes, the job and the car payments. The homeless guy just smiles. So tell me again; who's crazy? If, as some believe, everyone is where they are by choice, it begs the question.

With the mentally ill, those choices may not be there. Depending upon the illness, some decisions are just not within the realm of the possible.

One of the most common diagnosis' of the mentally ill homeless is schizophrenia. Despite some popular conceptions, schizophrenia is not the same as dissociative identify disorder, more commonly known as multiple personality disorder. Sybil wasn't a schizophrenic.

The world of a schizophrenic is distorted. Depending upon the level of affliction, his reality may be bent by hallucinations and delusions of any and all kinds. He may hear voices. He may feel things physically touching him. He may smell strong odors that exist nowhere other than in his own mind. He may actually see things you and I can't see. Every experience of the schizophrenic is just as real as any in the reality we inhabit.

Schizophrenia usually doesn't exhibit itself until early adulthood. If it strikes, it will almost always appear before the age of thirty. It may be slightly earlier in men than in women, but the years of susceptibility are generally between eighteen and thirty.

A standard for classifying schizophrenia recognizes three major types, paranoid, disorganized or hebephrenic and catatonic type. Paranoid schizophrenics may suffer from severe delusions and hallucinations, but otherwise may be clear thinking and logical. Catatonics may seem to be in a stupor, unable or unwilling to move or they may show signs of agitation and illogical and purposeless movements and motions.

Hebephrenic schizophrenics may suffer from severe delusions and hallucinations, but also exhibit an inability to maintain a logical train of thought. They may jump from topic to topic while mixing reality with their own delusions. Hebephrenic's written communications will show the same incoherent thinking and inability to stay on track.

Hebephrenic behavior can be so disorganized as to make employment impossible. Normal functioning is so impaired that hebephrenics may be unable to prepare meals, bathe or dress appropriately. It is not uncommon to find them dressed with many layers of clothing even on a warm summer day.

According to experts at the Mayo Clinic, hebephrenics may lack emotional expression. Facial expressions may be blank. They avoid eye contact and suppress body language. They want social isolation. Surprisingly, another common effect of being a hebephrenic schizophrenic is chain smoking. It is not uncommon for hebephrenics to die from heart or lung disease as a consequence of heavy smoking. Schizophrenics in general have life expectancies of ten to fifteen years less than the general population.

The debilitating effects of schizophrenia mean that a search for famous schizophrenics yields only a short list. Nobel Prize winning mathematician John Nash was the subject of the compelling movie *A Beautiful Mind*. Author Jack Kerouac was diagnosed in the Navy although he later claimed he faked the condition to win a discharge from military service. Musicians seem to dot the short list of well known schizophrenics. Syd Barrett of Pink Floyd, percussionist James Beck Gordon, Peter Green of Fleetwood Mac, trumpeter Tom Harrell, Bob Mosely and others suffered from the disease. The over representation of noted musicians seems to correlate with drug use, one of the suspected triggers of schizophrenia. Thanks to another outstanding cinematic effort, Benjamin Ayers was made famous by Steve Lopez in *The Soloist*. Ayers is a Julliard trained cellist who lived on the streets of Los Angeles suffering from schizophrenia. A number of experts in the field suggest that some of history's most famous religious figures were schizophrenics. After all, they were hearing voices and having visions of things others couldn't see.

One of the more colorful schizophrenics in our nation's history was Emperor Norton the First. Joshua Abraham Norton came to San Francisco at the time of the great California gold rush in the mid-nineteenth century. He enjoyed a fairly successful business career until the onset of his mental illness.

In 1859, Norton proclaimed himself "Norton I, Emperor of the United States". A local newspaper published his proclamation as a lark. One thing led to another and his claim took hold and grew for years. He wandered the streets of San Francisco dressed in his emperor's garb complete with gold epaulets, a saber and scabbard at his side and a high feathered hat befitting a man of his royal standing.

Citizens and government officials bowed to Emperor Norton and referred to him as "your majesty". Nearby California cities competed for his attentions and asked him to review military parades and events. San Francisco merchants relished the idea that the Emperor wore their clothes or ate in their establishments. If he did, a sign appeared in the window claiming "By

His Majesty - Emperor Norton I

Appointment of Emperor Norton I" and business pointed upward. Mark Twain and other famous writers mentioned Emperor Norton. Robert Lewis Stevenson made him a character in one of his novels. Norton became one of San Francisco's most famous tourist attractions in the city's early years.

Emperor Norton abolished Congress, issued money, eliminated old laws and wrote new ones. To this day, San Francisco brags of Emperor Norton's contributions to the city's rich history. There are plaques on the streets of San Francisco. Hotels have public rooms dedicated to Emperor Norton. When he died in 1880, thousands marched in his funeral procession and the city buried him in a millionaire's grave.

Emperor Norton may have been America's first schizophrenic to be embraced by his neighbors and his community. But he was not to be the last.

Chapter Six
The Sea Word

Our time in Arizona's White Mountains went with clock-like precision. We announced the sale of the real estate company to the agents, employees and the local newspaper. The evening following the public announcement, a steady stream of friends, old and new, came by the house to raise a glass of Dom Pérignon and bid Liz and me farewell on our world travels. I worried that Liz would wake up the following morning and realize the company she had poured heart and soul into for twenty-five years was gone and she would feel lost and empty. Her life had been so tied to building the community's most successful company, there had to be a piece of empty somewhere in her heart when the sun rose on "The Mountain".

After nearly a quarter century living and working together, I should have known better. She woke up the next morning full of enthusiasm and vigor looking forward to the future. The past would always be there to remember when time permitted. Today, we had to prepare for tomorrow.

Our sailing plans had solidified somewhat. We would depart the marina in Point Loma and casually sail south along the coast of Baja California spending a few days here and a few days there. We'd stock ship's stores in Cabo San Lucas, sail north to La Paz and spend some time in one of our favorite ports. Depending upon how much time remained before hurricane season, we would either loop north in the Sea of Cortez or sail three days directly across to Mazatlan, another of our favorite ports. Next to San Blas, Puerto Vallarta, Manzanillo and more port hopping until we reached the southern coast of Costa Rica where we would spend the hurricane season. Finally off to Los Cocos, islands blanketed in dense rain forest a few hundred miles south of Costa Rica. Our last planned destination would be the Galapagos Islands where we would walk in the footsteps of Charles Darwin. At that point, it would be decision time. On to the South Pacific or back through the Panama Canal and into the Caribbean for the following year. We were excited and ready to go.

With only a couple of weeks left for final goodbyes and last minute details standing between us and the open ocean, I received a phone call. It was from an old friend who had risen to become the head of the software empire for a Fortune 200 company. He wanted to get together and talk about "doing something" with my software company. When I hung up the phone, I told Liz he wanted to strike up some kind of marketing alliance and that I'd agreed to meet with him in Los Angeles the following week. Liz didn't miss a beat.

"They want to buy the company," she said.

A wistful grin took hold of my face and I said, "That would be nice, but I'm sure you're dreaming."

She just smiled and said, "I'm telling you . . ." She cut her words short.

Two days later, we walked into a conference room on a giant corporate campus in L.A. My friend and two of his assistants sat across the table from Liz and me. After a few pleasantries, Mike said, "We're currently expanding into the software world and are thinking it might be a good thing for us to form an alliance with your company. Depending upon your desires, it could even include the possibility of us buying a portion or even all of your company."

I tried not to appear anxious, but explained we were headed out to sea for a couple years and a purchase might be wise for all parties. We discussed the company's finances at some length and ultimately came to the topic of price. We agreed to write our respective estimates of the company's value on paper and lay them on the table. When the papers were unfolded, each had the exact same – to the penny – number written on them. We had a deal. The return trip to Arizona was an exercise in handling euphoria.

The successful sale of two substantial companies set us free to sail the world unencumbered by any commitments. We were truly free to go wherever our dreams and the wind took us.

Back in Arizona, we celebrated our great fortune with friends and family. Finally, as the day of departure was nearly upon us, Liz went in for a routine physical examination. It was three-thirty in the afternoon, less than sixteen hours from our long awaited exit. The doctor called Liz into his office and told her she had to come back the following day for more tests. Liz let him know she wasn't coming back for two years. She was leaving on a round the world sailing adventure the next morning.

"I found a suspicious spot on your mammogram," the doctor said with an earnest tone. "You need to have a biopsy."

Only women that have ever heard a similar statement can begin to understand the heavy, dead weight that descends upon the spirit. Emotions well up. Anger and fear and confusion tussle with each other in a mind that is suddenly racing faster than thoughts can be processed.

"If it's anything to worry about, we spotted it early. It's small," he said in an attempt to comfort the patient. Liz insisted she would not stay on The Mountain for the procedure, but agreed to arrange for the test in Scottsdale within the next couple of days. The next morning with apprehension decorated with enthusiasm, we said goodbye to the White Mountains and left for Point Loma via Scottsdale.

We had reason for optimism. The spot was small. There are plenty of "false positives" that do nothing other than torment women with the fear of breast cancer. Liz's own sister went through the same thing and it proved to be nothing. We viewed it as a minor delay. But we acted with haste and a sense of purpose in arranging for the tests. We worked our way into the schedule of the finest breast specialist in Arizona.

The biopsy was performed. The many possibilities and alternatives were explained in infinite detail. We were told it would take a couple of days to get the results. The woman whose personalized license plate reads "PERSIST" wasn't about to waste time waiting around for what we believed would be favorable results. We left the next morning bound for Point Loma and the sailing vessel Tempest.

We pulled into the village of Point Loma around 3 pm. It was sunny with wisps of fog from the ocean tickling the crest of the ridge of Point Loma. The smell and taste of the salt air was refreshing and welcome. The Mayor sat on his bench watching a theater of the mind on a distant stage. We went to the boat and busied ourselves by waiting.

Chapter Seven
The Mayor's New Neighbors

Even in stormy weather, there's an indescribable peacefulness to sleeping on the boat. On most nights, the gentle rocking, the water softly lapping the hull like a metronome, the occasional creak of the rigging and the glint of the moon reflecting off the water all come together in a great comforter that calms the soul. That night, we both pretended to sleep neither admitting to the other the burden of worry we carried. The morning walk started earlier than usual.

The Mayor's office sat empty in the dim pre-dawn light. A block later, we crossed Cañon Street. I looked to the west and saw the Mayor a couple blocks away working his way down the hill with a steady, purposeful pace, duffle bag over his shoulder.

"Here comes the Mayor," I said, "Right on schedule."

We'd seen him coming from that direction before and concluded he must have a room nearby. If he did, however, it was not equipped with laundry facilities. His clothes had grown progressively more seasoned with each passing day.

We kept on walking and kept on wondering about the strange man we called the Mayor. An hour later, we arrived at the deli and ordered breakfast. We sat outside at the same table we'd had the first time we ever saw the Mayor. A hundred feet away, he sat on his bench looking away from us.

It was another perfect Point Loma morning and we relaxed over a second cup of coffee surrounded by the flowers that make the village a year round Garden of Eden. It would have been a perfect morning in a perfect world. Liz's cell phone rang.

Liz seized the phone like a cat on a mouse. It was Dr. White calling from Scottsdale. Try as I might, I couldn't hear the words being said, but I could see the facial muscles in Liz's face grow tense. I looked away, perhaps for the same reasons the Mayor always looked away. Maybe my mind was suffering from an overload of thought and looking blankly into the distance lightened its load.

Liz closed her phone and put it down. She took a breath and said, "Shit. It's malignant. I have breast cancer."

In a moment's time, the course of our lives took a dramatic turn. There would be surgery, radiation, possibly chemo-therapy and if all went well, long term treatment. It was as if the vase that held the genie had just fallen from its place and shattered. Along with ten thousand pieces of porcelain and debris laid the wreckage of our dreams. Sailing vessel Tempest was staying in port indefinitely. In a flash, our wish of sailing around the world had vaporized like the morning mist burning off the ocean. We lost our wish of good health. Hopefully, it was a three wish genie we'd just set free from the bottle. We desperately needed one last wish – a speedy and complete conquest of the disease.

We continued our morning walks even as we spent our days visiting doctors and testing labs. The woman with the "PERSIST" license plate and the man who'd conquered some of the world's highest mountains weren't about to take a passive approach to dealing with the disease. After the diagnosis was validated, surgery was scheduled in less than a week. Liz was home the same night. The following week, radiation therapy began. There followed a lengthy period of regular monitoring, medication, tests, tests and more tests. But even with all the turmoil and disruptions, we reoriented our lives, reset our goals and smiled and laughed as much as we ever did. Happiness is a choice to be made rather than a consequence of our circumstances. How foolish would we be to choose the alternative?

The Mayor continued to choose the bench on the corner. San Diego weather is predictable, but not nearly as consistent and predictable as the Mayor. "We're going to be here for a long time," I told Liz. "Let's see if we can get him to acknowledge our existence. Don't you think it would be good if we existed? Maybe he can help us confirm our existence."

"You're as crazy as he is," Liz offered in support.

I was in the mood for a little mind-sport. "Remember Descartes said, 'I think, therefore I am.' Let's try to improve upon that. I say if he waves, therefore we exist."

Liz gave me one of her "you're the nut-case" smiles and I looked toward the Mayor. When I thought he might be glancing my way, I raised my arm and waved at him. He looked off in the distance and remained invisible. We walked on as usual talking about the Mayor, the boat, the weather and all of the world's problems.

The next day, as we walked past the Mayor's office, I waved a greeting and we continued on our way. The following morning we waved again. This went on for weeks with no response from the Mayor. Our discussions sometimes centered on the question of our existence. "He waves, therefore we exist," chuckled Liz. "It's looking like we may have a major problem."

We couldn't prove the Mayor could see us or if he could, if he noticed my waves. If he saw me wave did he know it was the same person each time? If he did, maybe he questioned my sanity thinking I was some crazy guy compelled to wave every day. We had a lot of unanswered questions, not the least of which was "Do we exist?"

The Tempest sat in her slip like a race horse ready to run. She was outfitted for a circumnavigation of the world. As sailing ships go, she was luxurious, roomy comfortable. As full time homes are concerned, she was a boat. The change in our life circumstances meant we had some new issues to resolve, not the least of which was "where did we live?"

Although we still owned a house high in the mountains of Arizona and another one in the desert resort town of Scottsdale, we had planned on making our ocean home, the Tempest, our place of residence for at least a couple of years. But that was to be out to sea and in an interesting, diverse series of enchanting ports of call. There we sat on a wonderful, but under-utilized yacht. Even an occasional week long junket to Ensenada, Mexico or Catalina Island couldn't shake the stigma that our race horse had become a barn-borne stable mare.

We could return to one of our homes in Arizona, but in truth, we had left Arizona mentally, emotionally, physically and spiritually. We had made the move to San Diego and we didn't want to look back. The marina the Tempest called home had many "live-aboards". Some of them would rise every morning, put on their three-piece suits and leave for their nine-to-five jobs in the financial section of the city. We could make the Tempest our full time home, but something was too unsettling about the prospect.

Some evenings, we would sit on deck, sipping a glass of wine and looking up at the lights twinkling in the mansions tucked into the side of the rock ridge of Point Loma. It was a magical view, the kind Disney's animators would create. The soothing breeze of a summer night heightened the pleasure of looking at what could just as easily have been the Amalfi Coast of Italy. I had spent a number of years living in San Francisco. It was reminiscent of the view of Sausalito glimmering at the foot of the Golden Gate Bridge.

"Maybe we should look for a house up there," I said barely above a whisper. I waited for Liz to talk some sense, but she was silent. The last time this happened, we ended up buying a yacht.

The following day, we were driving around the La Playa section of Point Loma looking at homes. We weren't interested in buying one; we were just curious to know what they cost. When we drove by one that was close to the village, we saw the sign that said "Open House". Below the sign hung another one boasting an "Ocean View". Knowing this wasn't possible for a home so close to the village itself, we stopped in to see what manner of slight-of-hand the seller was trying to perpetrate on the unsuspecting public.

We took possession of our new home six weeks later. The view included the skyline of the downtown, the San Diego Bay, Tijuana, Mexico, the Tempest sitting in her slip, the Point Loma peninsula and to the south and west, Mexico's Coronado Islands and the Pacific Ocean beyond. We lived on the boat while the house was gutted and rebuilt. The confrontation with cancer reminded us life is finite and if you wait too long for your dream, you may never see it come to life. Liz had a lifelong love affair with cooking and she was to have her dream kitchen. It took the contractor nearly a year to complete the mother of all kitchens with eleven prep stations and every tool, toy and gadget any chef could ever hope for. I'd rather die with debt than regret.

We officially became full-time Point Loma residents. The village of Point Loma was our yard and garden, the Mayor our monarch. We lived within a few hundred feet of his royal office.

Chapter Eight
More Questions than Answers

In a period of less than two years, I'd gone from world circling mountain climber, to ocean trekking sailor, to semi-sedentary land-lubber. The occasional medical trip gave us a welcome diversion into the desert, but for the most part, life involved a once-in-a-while two or three day trip on the boat, a periodic trip to Europe or Latin America and a lot of becoming a "normal" Point Loma resident. Of course the morning walks never stopped.

I kept waving to the Mayor every morning and some afternoons for nearly two months. He had become accustomed to ignoring me and I had grown accustomed to being ignored. But I learned long ago that you're never beaten until you quit playing the game. I continued to wave a greeting each time I passed him by.

One morning, the Mayor sat in his customary location holding court for subjects only he could see. One hand held his cigarette; the other lay casually along the back of his bench. When I thought I may have caught his eye, I launched my customary morning greeting. At

Mayor Pastorino rests in his "office"

first I thought I had imagined it, but he had actually raised his hand toward me and given me a tepid wave. His arm never separated from the bench; only his hand from the wrist flicked upward in an act of what would prove to be camaraderie.

"Incredible," I said. "He waved. We actually exist."

"Get outta here," said Liz. "Are you sure?"

"I'm as serious as the gout," said I. The rest of the morning walk was an exercise in managing elation. It had been years since I began wondering what was inside the head of the Mayor. What made him tick? How could he possibly be content to sit in the same spot day after day, month after month, year after year? On this day, as hyperbolic as it may seem, it was as if I'd been tapping on his door forever and finally someone on the other side was at least looking through the peep-hole to see who was knocking.

The following morning with the Mayor in his customary position, I waved as I had the day before. To my surprise, I got a full armed wave. He then looked away. With my curiosity burning, he'd given me another clue to his world. He recognized us and after a long period of time finally included us, even if only on its edges, as part of his world. We silently exchanged greetings for the next three weeks.

One morning as I approached, I glanced toward the Mayor's office to see if he was looking our way. He waved first, another milestone. Silly as it may sound, I felt as if I had a new friend. I never saw him initiate any kind of social contact with another human being. I actually felt special.

As time passed, we felt increasingly at home in Point Loma. We were discovering that despite the fact it was technically a part of San Diego, one of the largest cities in California, it was more like a very small town. We were meeting more of our neighbors in La Playa. They presented us with a diversity of cultures, education, social standing and backgrounds.

Marcie Rothman is a noted California food critic and author. We met her at a beach birthday party for a sailboat live-aboard friend we knew from the docks. I had just finished arguing with animal expert,

Joan Embery on the subject of who Joan Embery was while not realizing I was speaking with Joan Embery at the time. Marcie walked up and said, "What did you think of Joan Embery?" I laughed out loud when I discovered the folly of my ways. It had been some years since I'd seen her on the Johnny Carson show. She'd matured a little and I hadn't recognized her.

When Marcie and Liz got to talking and discovered they had a mutual love for cooking, fine dining and rare wines, they immediately hit it off like sisters. I am the frequent beneficiary of their shared passion for food. We often get together and the two of them take command of either Liz's or Marcie's kitchen either of which would be the envy of most restaurant chefs.

At one of these elegant dinners, I mentioned to Marcie that the Mayor had started waving to us as we passed him every day. "First, it was with just a flick of the wrist. Now it has grown into a full fledged wave," I said grinning.

"Oh, wow," said Marcie. "It sounds like you're probably his best friend."

We told her about our burning curiosity. "How can someone sit in the same place day in and day out? What can possibly be running through his head?" we asked. Little did we know that another big piece of the story was about to be revealed.

"You know his family lives right up the street from you," said Marcie. She said she heard it from a reliable source, a good friend of hers. The Mayor wasn't an accountant after all. He was just a crazy guy whose family couldn't do anything for him other than let him sit on his bench. The family was very well off, but no amount of money can buy sanity. They just let him live his life the way he wanted to live, sitting on the bench. They would occasionally bring him a new coat and shoes and give him money, but beyond that there was little else they could do for him.

Marcie had lived in the neighborhood for more than ten years. She should know the story if anyone did. "His name is David," she said. "I don't remember his last name."

Her story made sense. I remembered a couple months back, there had been a power failure around midnight. I looked outside to see if the lights were out in other homes or was the outage restricted to just our house. There was the Mayor walking up our street, his bag on his shoulder and his hood over his head. He must have been headed toward his parent's home.

The rumor about the Mayor being a CPA was apparently just that, a rumor. He was merely a local aberrant whose family was living with the albatross of a mentally ill child who had passed his entire adult life sitting on a bench near his parent's home. The explanation gave me some closure, but did nothing to give me insight into the machinations of his mind. What was in there? Maybe I could find his family and tactfully ask them. Marcie said she'd try and get the family's name. She never could.

The waves continued. There was no facial expression, just a simple wave between two acquaintances. With each passing day we became more familiar with the Mayor's habits and routine. The Village Store was directly across the street from the Mayor's office. For twenty two years, the market had been owned by a family of Iraqi immigrants cutting their piece of the American pie in Point Loma. We discovered the Mayor would dart across the street to purchase his cigarettes and food. He sometimes would leave his duffel on his bench. Even though he'd return within a minute or so, the duffel was never taken or bothered by anyone else. We suspected the Mayor's non-attention to hygiene may have afforded him a level of protection not shared by most. I know we certainly had no desire to approach the bag. We preferred to enjoy the aroma of the jacaranda flowers that lined the street.

Across Rosecrans from the Mayor's office was Gus' Pizza. We discovered he would sometimes hurry across the street, order a piece of pizza and scurry back to his office to enjoy his meal. We also learned he always had cash for his purchases. We'd see him stuffing it back into his coat pocket after one of his shopping runs.

Slowly, we were putting together the story of the mysterious homeless man. But for every question we answered, three more appeared. We learned that he would get a new hooded coat and boots every four or five months. Where were they coming from? He would often turn toward the rear of the bench and write things on a piece of paper. What was he writing? Where was he getting his cash? Where did he go at night? But above all else, our morning walks focused on the question of what was going through his mind? What thought processes allowed him to sit year after year in precisely the same spot?

Chapter Nine
Breaking Bread

We'd seen George walking along Shelter Island Drive occasionally. He was another sailboat live-aboard. One day at the post office, he approached us. "You have a sailboat, don't you?" he asked. He must have seen us on the docks.

"Have you got a drogue? If not you definitely need one." We explained we just happened to be in the market for a good drogue or as they're sometimes called, a sea parachute. Drogues are tethered to the helm in those hopefully rare times in which you encounter extreme weather at sea. The purpose is to slow the boat down in turbulent seas to prevent it from burying the bow in a wave trough and pitch-poling or flipping the boat. As we would later learn, by the time you really need one, it's almost too late. The seas become so rough it's nearly impossible to safely maneuver above deck without getting tossed overboard yourself. George manufactured sea drogues and sold them at trade shows around the country. He must have seen an easy sale when he spotted us in the post office and invited us back to his boat to pick our favorite.

Back at the docks, the conversation wandered from drogues to sailing to living on a boat. "Well, I guess it's better than living on a bench," said George.

I glanced his way and said, "Are you talking about that guy that's always sitting up on Rosecrans?"

"Yea," said George. "He's a head case, but he's alright. He's been there for years. He came to Point Loma to work in the boat yards and spent too much time inhaling the fumes of the paint he was putting on the boats. It did his brain in and he's been sitting on the bench ever since. He lives off of his disability pay from the insurance company. He never bothers anybody; he just sits there."

George said his name was Barry and he used to live in Florida. When I said I'd heard he was a CPA and had left his family, George just shook his head. "I also heard he was the son of some rich family up on the hill," I said.

George paused and looked at me and said, "You better check your sources," he said, "I heard it from a friend of mine who knew."

It seemed I was losing ground on my quest to understand the Mayor. The more I knew, the less I knew. He was a family man, a CPA, a boat yard worker, a mentally ill child of a rich, local family. Someone even suggested he was totally "normal" and was doing research for his Ph.D. in psychology. His name was David or Barry or Bob or the Mayor. All I knew then was that he was definitely suffering from multiple personality disorder, but unbeknownst to him, the personalities had been created by well intentioned gossip mongers in the community. The only thing the neighbors seemed to agree on was that he was some crazy guy that sat on the bench every day. Beyond that, there were nearly as many stories as there were neighbors. I thought someone knows the true story and that guy was sitting right in front of me.

The next morning, we walked the "Liberty Station" route. Point Loma offers plenty of eye candy to walkers willing to brave the hills and traffic. We try to vary our scenery every morning. Some mornings we walk along the San Diego Bay with its waters lapping the shores of Shelter Island. Other days begin with views of the surf of the open Pacific relentlessly beating the cliffs in Ocean Beach. We sometimes walk the ridge leading to Cabrillo National Monument. Dozens of red crowned parrots screech above us as we stare out at one of the most breathtaking views in California. The Liberty Station route is one we commonly take when we want to stop at the local grocery store and return along the commercial fishing docks in America's Cup Harbor. In the summer months, we step over the catch of the many sport fishermen that love to land the big tuna and other game fish common off the coast of Point Loma.

It's nearly two miles from our home along Rosecrans to Liberty Station. The route is dotted with commercial fishing and marine businesses, boutique hotels, restaurants, banks and a fortune teller. We passed the Mayor as usual and exchanged what had by then become the customary wave. For the rest of the walk, Liz and I talked about the identity of the Mayor. Most people agreed he was "the crazy guy" on the bench, but beyond that he remained a mystery.

"What if we just go up and talk to him?" I suggested to Liz. Her concern was that over the years we had observed him, we'd never actually seen him engage in any form of human interaction. He always tried to avoid contact with anyone. We had seen him when on rare occasions a stranger walked into his office and sat on one of the two vacant benches. He never looked directly at the person, but became agitated. He would stand up and nervously pace about. If the person didn't leave quickly, he would throw his duffel over his shoulder and go stand across the street looking stressed until the intruder departed. He would then return to his office and assume his customary position sitting on the bench looking off into the distance smoking his cigarette.

Liz was afraid that if just the mere presence of a stranger in his little area caused him so much stress, a direct confrontation might push him over the edge.

"Hey, it might be worth a shot," I said. "After all, we are best buddies. He doesn't wave to just anyone, does he?"

We kicked the idea around as we walked. The Mayor was obviously not Mr. Average and we really didn't have much knowledge of mental illness or homelessness. As we approached Harbor Drive, we picked up a whiff of grease in the air. The breeze was from the bay and for about a block when walking the Liberty Station path, we'd endure the smell of Winchell's Donuts. As tasty as their donuts may be, I hadn't set foot in a place like that for more than thirty years.

They weren't known for serving the type of food mountain climbers ate to maintain peak physical conditioning.

I veered to the left and with Liz looking on in amazement walked into Winchell's. I glared into the display case. When asked what I would like, I pointed to a big, glazed bear claw. "I'll have one of those," I said.

"What about your wife?" asked the clerk. She'd seen us walk by for a couple of years and assumed we were a matched set.

"It's not for me," I responded. "It's for a homeless guy down the street."

She grinned. "Oh, sure it is," she winked. She put the roll in a bag and Liz and I were soon on our way. It was about six blocks from Winchell's to the Mayor's office and we wondered how he would react.

At that time of the morning, the Mayor usually sat facing south. As we got within a block of his office, we saw he was sitting as expected looking away from us with the smoke from his cigarette snaking its way into the morning air.

When climbing mountains, there are times you have to cross over a crevasse by walking carefully over a snow bridge, a precarious arch of snow hanging in thin air over the bottomless crack in the glacier that could end up being the last thing you remember of this life. You expect the crossing to be successful and normal, but you know anything could happen. You prepare for the worst, hope for the best. When you arrive on the other side, there's a sense of great relief and a completely different view of your world. As I approached the "crazy guy on the bench", I felt as if I were taking that first step out on the snow bridge. I hoped for the best.

We made a wide loop from behind, not wanting to startle him. Liz stayed about twenty feet back. I agreed with her suspicion that it would be better for just one of us to approach him. We didn't want to risk making him feel like we were double-teaming him and cause him to react with paranoia and run.

When I got about ten feet away from him, I intentionally cleared my throat to make some noise. The hood on the jacket quickly wheeled around and revealed the weathered face of the Mayor looking directly at me. His eyes sliced into me from within the hood and betrayed a look of mixed surprise and concern from the intrusion.

I held up the Winchell's bag with the bear claw half sticking out the top. "Would you like a donut?" I asked. As I spoke, I could see he recognized me as the guy he'd been waving to for the past few months. His face suddenly relaxed noticeably, but he didn't smile.

"Yea. That would be good," he said. "Thanks."

I handed him the bag. "You're welcome," I said and I turned and walked on toward the house. We waited until we'd walked another block before we sneaked a glance back toward the Mayor. He was in his normal morning sitting position, hood covering his head, looking off toward the south and eating his donut. We felt like we'd crossed the bridge and the strange bonds of friendship had strengthened again.

Thursday morning dawned cooler than normal. Fall was in the air. We walked by and waved. He waved in return.

Friday, I stopped at Winchell's. A super-large glazed cinnamon roll was $1.29. The clerk asked again if I wanted something for Liz and she scoffed again when I said it wasn't for me. We walked the six blocks toward the Mayor's office wondering if the response would be similar to Wednesday's or would he be sitting on a different branch of his boingo-boingo tree. Even though we had established a relationship with him, he was still "the crazy guy on the corner." We didn't know what to expect.

"How about a cinnamon roll," I said as I came up from behind.

He jumped, a little startled. When he saw it was me, his face relaxed. "Yea, sure," he said. "That sounds good. Thanks."

It became a regular ritual. Usually about twice a week, I'd bring him a donut. The other days, we just exchanged greetings. Liz would hang back twenty or so feet during the donut transfer so as to not make him feel like we were overpowering him. We felt privileged that the Mayor was sharing his life with us even if it was in just some small way. This human being that no one seemed to know was proving to be an interesting and friendly person. Never once did he ask for anything. Never once did he not express his gratitude when he was given something. He never developed any outward sign of expectation. He wanted to be left alone, but when approached by someone who had no desire to cast judgment, he was a friendly, normal kind of a guy. Over the entire term of the relationship, it remained pure in the sense that there was no quid-pro-quo. Nothing was asked. Nothing was demanded. Nothing was expected. There were only gifts of friendship, a simple wave, a warm word, an expression of gratitude and a respect for each other's worlds. If only more of my "normal" friends were as normal as the crazy guy on the bench. And the woman at Winchell's never believed he existed.

Chapter Ten
Getting to Know You

Our relationship with the Mayor evolved rapidly once we learned we could engage him in conversation. We would have liked to have invited him to dinner at the house and sit and chat with him about his history, his views and the reasons he sat on the bench every day, but there were a number of obstacles to this approach. Our house has plenty of windows and the afternoon ocean breezes ventilate the house well, however, not well enough to endure dinner with someone whose hygiene calls for a bath only when the rains provide one. I'll confess that in my mountain climbing days, we'd sometimes go for weeks without a bath, but it was forty below zero. I'm not sure if the nose quits functioning in those conditions or if odors just freeze and shatter like glass before they get to the nose. We weren't thoroughly disgusting until we returned to civilization longing for a shower and a cold beer. The Mayor was, by homeless people's standards, quite well kempt, fastidious and meticulous. But to qualify for a seat in our dining room he would have had to be driven through the car wash a couple of times. We didn't think we had yet become close enough friends to ask him to suffer that indignity.

Another obstacle was the fact that he was still the crazy guy on the bench. He was friendly with us and welcomed us into his world of invisibility and mystery, but he hadn't adopted us as kin folk. Frankly, Liz and I were also a little concerned that if he knew where we lived, we could have some unanticipated difficulties. We were expert on neither homelessness nor mental illness. We wondered how we would react if we returned from one of our trips to Arizona only to discover the Mayor had moved into our smoke-free house and was lighting one cigarette after another while lounging in the big leather chair in the living room. We really didn't expect it, but then we never would have expected someone to sit for years in the same spot.

We opted for an approach of more of the same. We intended on continuing our walks and we knew he wasn't going anywhere. We had all the time in the world and would gradually learn what we could one little snippet at a time. Winchell's Donut shop would become a regular stopping point on our morning walk.

One evening, Liz and I were dining at an Italian restaurant a block from the Mayor's office, the same one where the owner had told me the Mayor was just "some crazy guy" that was always sitting on the bench. It was in the fall and the darkness crept upon us a little earlier every night. We were in the mood for a dessert. As we waited for the dessert menu, I happened to glance in the direction of the Mayor's office. I could still see him sitting in his usual location.

"We'd like two orders of the hot bread pudding with ice cream," I said to Rob, the restaurant owner.

"Coming right up," he said.

Before Rob could walk away, I jumped in and said, "But we'd like one of them to go. And if you've got a plastic spoon, could you throw that in the bag too?"

He gave me a quizzical look. "It's for the Mayor," I said.
Rob waited for us to finish our dessert before bringing us the bill and the hot bread pudding and ice cream. "The Mayor's is on the house," he said with a smile.

When we got to the corner, the Mayor waved. "Do you like bread pudding and ice cream?" I asked.

With what seemed like a little more enthusiasm than normal, he said, "Oh yea. That sounds good."

I asked him if he had a spoon in his bag. He wasted no time digging it out. As we walked home we could see him savoring his evening treat in the shadows created by the streetlight above his office. A block later, we glanced back and he was gone.

The following morning would be the beginning of our discovery period. It seemed odd that for years, we'd had such intense curiosity about the Mayor and only now would we try and learn more from the source himself. We walked as usual. The Mayor was in his office as usual. The counter clerk at Winchell's again accused me of eating the roll, this time an apple fritter. Liz chimed in herself, "No really; it's for a homeless man down the street." The clerk looked unconvinced.

As always, the Mayor graciously thanked me. Before walking away, I said "By the way, you've never told me your name."

"Jeff," said the Mayor. He didn't share a last name. He was only Jeff. I wished him well, turned and headed for the house. Interesting, I thought to myself. The crazy guy on the bench didn't seem to know his own name. Marcie had assured us he was David, the son of a well-to-do Point Loma family. Maybe he had two names. Could he be "Jeff David"? Could Marcie be wrong? We wondered for the next week while we were in Arizona for Liz's regular medical checkup. By the time we returned to Point Loma I was determined to get to the bottom of the matter.

"How are you doing?" I asked the Mayor on my first morning back.

"Hi. How's it going?" he responded. We had known him long enough by this time that Liz had reduced her "safe distance" from twenty or so feet to a step or so behind me. She still didn't speak with him directly, but he seemed to feel comfortable enough with her being there. I explained to the Mayor that someone had told me his name was David and that he had family nearby. I asked him if that was true.

"No, my name is Jeff," he said.

"Has it always been Jeff?" I asked. He was emphatic and sincere and assured me it had never been anything but "Jeff". The nature of mental illness was a great curiosity to me, but surely he would know his own name and if it's ever been different.

I must have had a quizzical look on my face because after a couple seconds of silence, he said, "But you know, a person can actually become a different person if he wants to. It takes seven years. You have to bury your old clothes and you can't eat certain things for seven years and if you don't break any of the rules, then you become a completely different person."

It immediately became obvious that this direct discovery process wasn't going to be all I expected it to be. By going directly to the well spring, I now knew the Mayor's name is actually Jeff, not David and that it has always been Jeff except when he wasn't. It was sounding like being crazy was, if nothing else, a very entertaining sport. I hoped I was up for the game.

I worried a little that by questioning him about his identity, I may have damaged the trust we'd built up over the course of the past couple of years, but in the days that followed, everything seemed to be as normal as it had been. We didn't bring him breakfast or desserts every day. We didn't want to spoil the friendship by creating expectations that would yield to disappointments when not fulfilled.

By early December, we had shared a number of discussion topics. They were usually brief because Jeff seemed to have an ability to deviate from the topic in some creative ways. It was becoming clear he was a schizophrenic and subject to delusions that were as real to him as any experiences we've ever known.

We had dinner again at Luna Notte, the Italian restaurant famed for its bread pudding. Point Loma was decorated with the lights of the season and festive diners toasted the holidays and upcoming New Year. Illuminated by the soft light of Christmas decorations and passing cars, the Mayor could be seen working alone in his office.

He was leaning over the back of his bench scribbling notes on a piece of paper. We left the restaurant with his Christmas dessert in a bag.

When we approached, he jumped from his bench and came at us almost in a run. He was clearly agitated. It was worse than we'd ever seen him even when an intruder had invaded his space to sit on one of his benches.

"They're listening to everything we say," he said with a sense of urgency. He spoke in a low, but earnest voice. He explained the government agents had set up their listening devices on boats in one of the marinas nearby. From that point on, he stopped making a lot of sense. I already knew government agents were listening to us and reading our emails and of course they were also watching us; I'd just received a speeding ticket in the mail from Arizona after being photographed by one of the government's cameras. But Jeff's concern and level of excitement seemed disproportionately out of line. I didn't want to say anything that would cause him to suspect I thought that maybe his mental tires weren't inflated to the correct operating pressure. I was at a loss as to how to respectfully, but honestly, respond.

"That's really interesting," I muttered. "You should write that down." He went on some more about the men that were coming to track us. "Really," I said, "You should write all of this stuff down." I tried to look as serious and sincere as I could, but it was no easy task. Liz had already turned and walked across the street. I assumed to give Jeff and me privacy, but she later explained she couldn't keep a straight face any longer and didn't want Jeff to notice."

I bid the Mayor farewell and walked away hoping he'd take my advice and commit his thoughts to writing. It would make interesting reading in the future.

The more we got to know our friend the Mayor, the more we realized why so many people called him "the crazy guy on the bench." He was crazy and he always sat on the bench.

I never spent time pondering the meaning of the word "crazy", but my relationship with Jeff gave me reason to think about it regularly. Even to a lay person, it was increasingly apparent he was a classic schizophrenic. In a crass way of speaking, he was crazy. But he was a pensive, feeling, caring human being. He was gracious. He was reliable. He was trustworthy. And he was crazy.

How far are any of us from the bench? Is the kind of mental illness that afflicts the Mayor an all or nothing condition? Is there a switch somewhere in the mind that is either on or off? The more I learned about the Mayor the more it seemed improbable to me. Surely some people are more or less crazy than others. It seemed not only possible, but unavoidable to conclude that mental illness is a continuum. If it's true, then we're all a little bit crazy, some of us more than others.

At some point, our degree of craziness must reach a tipping point, a point at which we're no longer able to function within the normal confines of society. We can no longer hold a job, organize our lives or communicate with others effectively. When we reach the tipping point, our choices become limited. We may deal with the problem by finding a bench where the sun shines, but it's never too hot or cold. Maybe we'll sit on that bench. Maybe we'll sit there forever.

Christmas morning dawned cold and crisp. We knew the Mayor would soon arrive at his office on the corner. I left the house at the first sign of morning light. I placed a brightly decorated canister of cashews and a bag of homemade Christmas cookies topped with a bow on the Mayor's bench. He might be a crazy guy, but he was our crazy guy. We were on the same rock hurling through space. Someone had to care.

Throughout the following two and a half years, we continued to forge a stronger relationship with the Mayor. It goes without saying that the friendship was strange, but in some ways, it was the purest form of camaraderie. No one expected anything. No one demanded anything. No one asked for anything. Friendship was given and taken without preconditions.

Until we got to know him better, we wondered if he even noticed our absences. If we put out to sea for a week or if we traveled to Arizona for a week, did he miss our morning visits? As much to flatter ourselves with a sense of importance than to set his mind at ease, we would let Jeff know when we were going to be gone for more than a few days.

"Hey, buddy. You're in charge of Point Loma for a few days," we'd tell him. "We're going to Mexico. See you when we get back."

"OK," he'd say. "Have a good trip."

Not knowing how the mind of a crazy guy works, we didn't know if he spent his endless hours on the bench "thinking" about people, things and ideas or whether his time was largely passed in a trancelike state. The fact that he spent time writing meant he dwelled on the things that extended outside the realm of the immediate. What were they? To answer our question, we could only keep asking.

Our discussions touched on many topics as time went on, but the Mayor clearly had his favorites or his areas of specialty. He showed a lot of interest in business and finance. I remembered the stories of his past where he'd been a CPA or accountant. They seemed to be given merit by his frequent discussion of financial matters.

Before the crash of Bear Stearns and the financial world, the Mayor tipped me off on the impending doom. He let me know that although the public was generally in the dark on the subject, the banking world was controlled by a very small number of people. Jeff assured me they were setting up a collapse of the system. When it was over, there would be only a handful of banks remaining and that only the ultra-wealthy would be allowed to have accounts in these banks.

"Yea," said the Mayor, "Before they'll even let you open an account, you have to go in with a $100,000 bill."

"They won't let you have an account if you bring in two $50,000 bills?" I implored. He assured me it had to be a $100,000 bill.

By this time in our relationship, Liz was a fully fledged member of the inner circle. She no longer stood in the background, but she almost never engaged in the conversation. She just stood with us and took it all in. It had become clear Jeff was a "disorganized" or hebephrenic schizophrenic. It was always interesting to try and follow some of Jeff's scholarly dissertations because hebephrenics would start "on point" but often follow the path of a fireworks display in getting to their point. It could be a genuine test of will and self control to follow a discussion to its "logical" conclusion without having the jaw drop open or the eyes roll back in the head. The Mayor had become a dear friend and the last thing in the world we wanted to do was hurt his feelings, offend him or show him disrespect. We were guests in his world and we'd been brought up to show respect to our host.

Over time, Liz learned to signal her readiness to leave by turning her back to the conversation and looking off into the distance. I had learned this was her silent way of letting me know her jaw had dropped in stunned amazement or her eyes had rolled back in her head in nature's manner of saying, "Holy shit! Did you hear what he just said?"

When I learned a pair of $50,000 bills wouldn't open the door of the bank, I noticed Liz was staring toward the fog bank rolling in from the ocean.

"You ought to write all that down," I told the Mayor. "That is some really interesting stuff. Hey, gotta run. See you later."

As we headed toward the house, we pondered the possibility that the Mayor would have the presence of mind to long remember our discussion. Were these delusions as spontaneous in their dissipation as they were in their creation or were they part of the fabric of his reality? As was so often the case with Jeff, every little thing we learned produced more questions than answers. It wasn't clear if we were gaining or losing ground in our quest to understand him. The more we learned the more there was to learn. Maybe I was destined to sit on the bench myself reflecting on the mysterious until my head exploded and I disappeared. Actually, maybe that's how Jeff got there.

An ocean mist had dampened the ground the following morning, but the Mayor was in his office as usual. As we approached, his normally placid demeanor was gone. He was waving us over to the bench. He excitedly reached in his bag and pulled out a piece of paper. He said, "This is what I was talking about yesterday. You've got to have one of these before you can open an account in one of those banks."

He handed me a page he had ripped out of a magazine. It contained a picture of a $100,000 bill. The bill was real. It was printed in 1934 and carried the picture of President Woodrow Wilson. The crazy guy on the bench had continuity of thought. He could plan ahead and base his planning on past events. He was fully aware of his surroundings and events that he perceived as relevant to his world. Unlike many Americans, he also knew the $100,000 bill existed. And in his opinion, it would be required in the wake of an impending financial crisis. So who's the crazy guy? My broker didn't anticipate the magnitude of the crisis that was soon to strike the economy. In hindsight, the Mayor's prognostication was every bit as good as my broker's. "Thanks," I said. "That's really interesting. Catch you later." Liz had already turned her back and was ready to walk on.

On rare occasions, the Mayor would be absent from his office. Usually, he was on a quick trip to buy cigarettes or a sandwich or (we assumed) a bathroom visit. One cool, foggy Sunday morning we found another clue to the Mayor's world. The San Diego County Credit Union has a branch office close to our home. We turned the corner and came upon the Mayor standing at the ATM machine. We assumed he was withdrawing cash. We kept our distance; no one wants his space invaded as he's withdrawing cash from a bank. It seemed we'd answered the question of where the Mayor got his money. We knew he always had money; we had seen him pull a wad of bills from his pocket. He had to have money to buy his snacks and cigs and he certainly wasn't undernourished. He always carried a few extra pounds. He had access to a bank account.

Again, an answer yielded more questions. Was his wealthy family feeding the account? Was he independently wealthy himself and merely living on the investment income? Perhaps he was receiving some type of government assistance that was deposited directly into his account. Another event had poured fuel onto the fire of curiosity that burned within us.

Some may ask why we didn't just sit down with Jeff and ask him our growing list of questions. After all, how long could it take to run down the list? In truth, it would take many years. The Mayor was mentally ill. We had spent years gaining his trust, a trust that we honored and had grown to cherish. To sit down and interrogate him like a reporter or criminal investigator would have assuredly driven him into withdrawal and risked the destruction of a relationship that we enjoyed.

The biggest obstacle to a straight forward question and answer session came from one simple, insoluble fact; Jeff was a hebephrenic schizophrenic. If you asked him one simple question, his answer might start out logically enough, but more often than not it would involve a series of jumps each of which may have had nothing to do with the previous step and each of which may have been colored by a rather "creative" delusion.

About the time I met Jeff, I had been on the dock when a 140 foot mega-yacht was entering the slip adjacent to ours. High above on the deck of this magnificent, gleaming yacht stood a young woman who was obviously the junior deckhand. She was nervous and appeared to be inexperienced. The wind was blowing as the captain brought the yacht to a halt. Knowing time was of the essence, the deckhand was delighted to see me on the dock below. I waved to her to throw me the large, heavy dock line so I could secure the ship. It's always embarrassing, especially when there's a crowd watching, to throw the dock line and miss the dock. As it lands in the water, it magically splashes egg on the face of the person who threw it and who is now frantically pulling the line from the water in the hope the yacht is still within range when the line is ready to throw again. The young deckhand was visibly delighted when her throw proved to be perfect. I promptly grabbed the line and began securing it to one of the cleats on the dock. Her smile turned to chagrin as onlookers laughed when the entire dock line fell into the water. She had forgotten to tie the other end of the line to the boat. The wind that was now blowing her out into the bay muffled the sound of laughter, but failed to hide the red on her face.

That experience is similar to engaging in a structured conversation with a disorganized schizophrenic. You might be holding the line, but it is rarely secured at both ends. It can be the source of great entertainment, but the ship is adrift.

The Mayor was almost obsessed with health and nutrition. It struck us as odd that a person who received almost no exercise, was somewhat overweight, smoked like a fire in a rubber tire dump and lived in part on Winchell's donuts and bread pudding with ice cream could be so concerned with health and nutrition.

When dining out, we almost always walked to area restaurants. A multiplicity of dining choices is one of the great things about living close to the village of Point Loma. Despite our sometimes Herculean efforts, we weren't always able to finish the entire meal. In such cases, we'd ask for the "doggy bag" and see if the Mayor would like the remnant. "Yea, that sounds good. Thanks," he would say. There wasn't much he didn't like. He was always delighted with half of a chorizo burrito with jalapeños from Loma Bonita. He loved the pasta dishes from Luna Notte and later, Pomodoro. We learned he did not like sea food. His office was just a few short blocks from the shore and from Point Loma Seafoods, a fish lover's heaven on earth. He was like a kid in Candyland that didn't like sweets.

He would graciously thank us for steak, but we tried to avoid bringing him foods that required a lot of chewing. Whatever his health regimen may have been, it apparently didn't include good dental health. As near as we could see, he had no more than one or two teeth in his mouth. He regretted not having teeth, but his spirits were buoyed because he was in the process of growing them back. We didn't ever understand the details of the process, but it must have been a lengthy one. Over time, we never noticed any progress. Nonetheless, he remained faithful to his belief he was growing new teeth.

There were times when his attention to a healthy diet was so extreme you might have suspected him of being in training for the Olympics. In the aftermath of a health crisis, my 85 year old mother moved to Point Loma. She bought a condo a block and a half from the Mayor's office. When I was growing up, my mother thought Twinkies fell into the general category of "health food". In the years that followed, she upped her standards, but still suffers lapses occasionally. In a moment of impulse while at the grocery store, she purchased a large bag of popular corn chips. She didn't realize until she got home they were spiced with a Mexican pepper flavor. She thinks catsup is hot sauce. We stopped by one afternoon and she tried to give us the bag of chips.

"Thanks for the offer, but we don't eat things like that," Liz told her.

"Well, take them down and give them to the Mayor," she said. It seemed wasteful to throw food away even corn chips with more nourishment in the packing material than the chips themselves. We walked toward the Mayor's office with the bag of chips in hand.

He stood up to greet us. We handed the bag to him. "Thanks," he said. He held the bag up and squinted through his reading glasses to read the ingredients on the back of the package. He handed them back to me and said, "Thanks, but I can't eat these. Too much sodium. They're not very healthy." There was no way to ship them to the starving kids in China my mother used to tell me about when I was a kid, so the chips ended up in the trash.

The Mayor knew what to eat to cure a variety of health problems. One warm summer day, Jeff was sitting on the bench in his full regalia, hiking boots, coat, his hood up and telling us about the metal rod he had running directly from his heart to his gall bladder. He must have detected a hint of disbelief on my face because he felt compelled to say it again. He explained it developed as a result of an anesthetic "they" had given him some time in the past. It was uncomfortable and hurt him sometimes, but he knew how to control it. The secret was to eat cheese and broccoli soup. The combination of the cheese and broccoli somehow worked chemically to soften and dissolve the metal.

He also had to watch his diet to prevent antler growth. The first time he told us about this potential ailment, we thought he was kidding or worse yet, demonstrating he was capable of metaphor. But the more he explained, the more we realized he was absolutely serious. He was talking about physically growing antlers.

"Have you seen that other guy that walks around here sometimes?" he said. "He actually had to go to the doctor to have them removed." If only the guy had a copy of Jeff's diet, he could have avoided an office visit.

Jeff had a recurring problem with an itch on the back of his shoulder. It too was the result of the anesthetic "they" had given him. He said the sun really made it worse. We got the impression he may have been seriously sunburned at some time in the past, but we could never connect the dots.

The Mayor was meticulous in certain ways. He was always clean shaven. He would periodically groom himself in public. He would remove his shoes, trim his nails, and carefully clean his feet to maintain his hygiene all the while sitting on the bench in clothes that hadn't seen detergent in weeks. The ways of the Mayor were strange indeed.

Social interaction was rare. He had a long standing relationship with the people in the Village Store and Point Loma Drugs where he bought his essentials. There was one man that worked in a boat yard that would stop at Jack-in-the-Box and buy Jeff a breakfast meal from time-to-time, but we hadn't seen him in over a year. We suspected he'd left the area.

There was another homeless man that we nicknamed "the Teamster" that briefly invaded Jeff's office. Rather than rely on the standard grocery cart as his storage vehicle, the Teamster showed up one day at an intersection a half mile from the Mayor's office pulling a custom, tandem wagon complete with drawers and cabinets. His "rig" stood four feet high and was elegantly constructed. Like the Mayor, the Teamster would sit for days at a time in one spot. Unlike the Mayor, he would then get up and move to another location and spend a few more days.

The inevitable happened and the Teamster moved into the Mayor's office. It was strange to see the Mayor on his customary morning bench while his afternoon bench was occupied by a stranger. The Mayor spent much of the next three days in a state of agitation. He kept his back turned to the invader. The teamster actually spent most of his time sitting on the ground in front of the bench, but he was clearly deemed a space invader by the Mayor. He tried to behave as normally as possible when we brought him a cinnamon roll the next morning, but a furtive glance toward the Teamster seemed to serve as a statement from the Mayor: "You see? People are coming to see ME in MY space."

If at any time during the three day standoff there was conversation between the Mayor and the Teamster, we were unaware of it. On the fourth morning, the Teamster had moved on and Mayor Jeff had settled back into his routine of invisibility to all in the world but his friends. I stopped and struck up a conversation.

"Did you know that guy that was here?" I asked. "Didn't it bother you to have someone in your office?"

I could tell it did, but he remained calm as he explained. "It was just some guy from Loma Portal Elementary School. They sometimes like to come down here and take territory from the Cabrillo Elementary people."

There was a wild one. If I was to believe the Mayor, we'd just spent three days watching a turf war between elementary schools and fought between two guys each a half century old. Cabrillo Elementary School is across the street from our house so we were glad the Loma Portal guy lost the showdown. We also thought the Mayor's explanation tended to corroborate the story about him being the son of a well to do family in the village. If he grew up there then he would have probably gone to Cabrillo. But then why didn't more of the locals know him as someone other than "the crazy guy on the bench"?

Not all of the Mayor's social problems were as easily remedied. Liz and I were walking from the house to the marina one Saturday afternoon when we saw an ominous sign. Two police cars were at the corner of Rosecrans and Avenida de Portugal. We quickened our pace. As we got closer we saw two police officers confronting Jeff while two more stood back close to the curb. The Mayor remained seated on his bench, but his eyes betrayed a look of animal fear. One officer was asking him questions as we arrived. I walked directly in front of the police and put my hand on Jeff's shoulder. "How're you doing buddy? Everything OK?"

The Mayor looked up at me and said, "Yea, I'm OK."

I turned to the officers and said, "You know he's our neighbor, don't you? Jeff's lived here in Point Loma for a long time. He doesn't drink or do drugs of any kind. Is there a problem I can help with?"

"No, we're just questioning him. Someone from the bank on the opposite corner called and said he was sleeping here on the bench and we just came out to check on him." I assured them that he sat on the bench a lot and liked to close his eyes and relax there.

I turned to the Mayor and said, "Let me know if you need anything. See you later." As I turned and walked away I waved at one of the officers and asked to see her off to the side. She said everything would be alright. They just had to respond because of the call. I walked on periodically checking over my shoulder to make sure. The police drove off and the Mayor turned his back on the world and looked into infinity.

I had no way of knowing if a bank employee or customer called the police, but it wasn't the first time I learned of bank involvement with the Mayor. A year or two earlier, an item appeared on the Peninsula Community Planning Board's agenda. It simply said, "Homeless problem at the corner of Rosecrans and Avenida de Portugal." It was an obvious reference to the Mayor himself. I spoke with a representative from the board and was told the bank had sent a letter complaining about the increasing problem of homeless bums congregating at the corner and detracting from their business operation. I told the board member there was no truth to the allegation of an increasing problem and that I was certain no groups were congregating there. I then wrote a letter and sent it to the PCPB expressing displeasure with the agenda item. In the letter, I said I fully supported the board in its efforts to maintain community building and architectural standards, but that social engineering was beyond the purview of the board. I was assured they agreed with me and the item was removed from further consideration.

In the never ending search for clues into the nature of the man we called the Mayor, one other food story raised the hackles on my back. On one morning walk, we stopped at Vons, our local grocery store. They had just brought a tray full of freshly baked cheese bagels from the back room and were placing them in the bin. I thought to myself that if they taste half as good as they smell, the Mayor would probably love one. When we gave it to him, he thanked us and we walked home. The following morning, he made it a point to tell us how much he liked the bagel. It was rare we'd seen him with so much enthusiasm.

"Those are the best bagels in the world," he nearly danced as he spoke. Then for some reason, he felt compelled to tell us how they were made. "You know how they get the cheese inside the bagels?" he asked. He didn't wait for us to answer. "They have to shock it. They have to shock it to get it in there." As he spoke, his eyes widened as if to intensify the words. "They shock it to get it inside," he said again.

Chapter Eleven
Time Runs Out

When fall came to Point Loma in 2008, the Mayor had another new coat and shoes. "Hey, I see you've got a new coat. It looks great", I said.

His eyes beamed with pride. "Yea, thanks," he responded. "New shoes too."

"You're in charge of Point Loma for a month starting this weekend," I said.

"You leaving town?" he asked.

I told him we were going to England for a month. I looked at my friend and said, "Do you want me to bring you something from England?"

Jeff looked up at me pensively. He paused for a moment. "I don't know. What do they have?"

At first, I thought it was a strange question, but then I thought about what I would say if I had been asked what I wanted from England. What would I say? The Beatles? The Queen? Once again, the question on the table was "Who's the crazy one?"

Nearly four weeks later Liz and I stood in the entrance of Windsor Castle, the Queen's humble little thousand room weekend getaway. We thought of the Mayor and hoped all was well with him. I walked into the gift shop and found a writing pen emblazoned with the Queen's picture. I could now return to the United States and tell the Mayor they had a pen in England. He was delighted when he received his gift from the Queen.

The topic of discussion on one of our morning walks late that fall dripped with irony and sarcastic humor. We couldn't help but notice our relationship with the Mayor had become almost too normal. Was it our imagination or had he been changing in some ways in recent weeks? He seemed to be slimming down a little and taking better care of himself. On more than one occasion we had caught him at the laundry a block from his office. He wasn't comfortable spending time inside buildings, but he would get a machine loaded then grab a chair and take it out to the sidewalk to smoke and wait. It was as if having friends might have nudged him off his bench a little more.

"What if we've ruined the guy?" I asked Liz. "He's been a perfectly content crazy guy on the bench all of these years and now he's starting to go 'normal' on us."

"Maybe there's some public agency that can help in cases like this," Liz mused in jest.

Two weeks later, we walked by the laundry. We saw the Mayor sitting outside. "Hello," I said as I passed. "Taking care of laundry business?"

He looked up and greeted me with, "How's it going Colonel?"

Colonel?! My God, the Mayor had come up with a nickname for me. The world is coming to an end I thought. Liz suggested to me that only crazy people come up with nicknames for others. "Sort of like you when you named him the Mayor," she laughed.

All would not stay well in paradise forever. Despite the fact that Point Loma is on the ocean's edge and constantly cleansed with the cool, moist breezes, it technically remains a desert. In December, we had a cold spell punctuated with some rain. The Mayor sought cover beneath the façade of the Village Store, but was unable to stay totally dry and warm.

As we did every Christmas Day, we took some wrapped gifts and headed toward the Mayor's corner. He wasn't there. We returned and waited. Four or five trips throughout the day found an empty bench. He hadn't missed a Christmas Day in years.

When we arrived the next morning, cheese bagel in hand, he didn't look well. He took the bagel and thanked us in a raspy, labored voice. Not being a doctor, I couldn't say if he had a bad cold, the flu, pneumonia or a severe case of some mysterious jungle disease. Whatever it was, he looked like hell and sounded like the devil. I suggested to him that we could take him to the doctor, but he would have none of it. "I'll be OK," he said. "It's from the nuclear testing they did a few years ago."

We were relieved to learn he had recovered from his brief bout of normalcy, but we were concerned about his health. We kept a closer than normal eye on him for the next couple of weeks and he seemed to slowly recover. The illness had drained him of his energy. He was more lethargic than usual for many weeks afterward. Life did edge its way back to normal. He looked forward to his cheese bagels and we enjoyed our regular verbal forays into the worlds of business, health, people and whatever surprise topic might spontaneously be born of the mind of the Mayor.

As the dog days of summer approached Point Loma, the Mayor's office hours started to become erratic. He started showing up a little later than normal and was leaving a bit earlier. On one morning, we arrived well after his normal office opening time only to find his bench empty. I left the bag containing his bagel on the bench. The following morning we exchanged greetings and he thanked us for leaving the welcome treat for him. Somehow he looked different, maybe a little older.

A week or so later we walked by an empty bench two hours later than he routinely arrived. We worried about him and I walked up the street two or three times later that morning to see if he had arrived yet. Finally, I spotted him sitting on his bench. I walked up to him to say hi. "Hey, what happened? You were late for work today."

"I got up on the wrong side this morning," he said in a voice that conveyed a sense of discomfort. I looked down at his hands and they appeared to be swollen.

"You alright?" I asked.

"Yea, I'll be OK," he said as if questioning himself.

Over the years, we never wanted to invade his privacy so much as to ask him where he went to spend his nights. There were as many rumors about that as there were about his past. Some said he slept in the bushes near the school. Others said he actually had a room, but if he had one, it didn't come with laundry soap. I heard the priest at St. Agnes Catholic Church let him sleep in one of the buildings. I was fairly certain he slept outside and for years I knew he always walked down the hill on Cañon Street each morning. On our morning walks, if we didn't see him sitting on his bench, we would glance up Cañon as we crossed often seeing him with his duffel on his shoulder coming down the hill headed for his corner.

The morning of August 5th, he was late again. We scanned the hillside on Cañon and spotted him sitting on a bench. He had never done this before. A half hour later, he was at his post when we came by with a Winchell's bear's claw. He thanked us as he always did. He seemed to be in good spirits, but his hands were more swollen. "What's the matter with your hands?" I asked.

"Oh, nothing. I slammed it in a door when I was a kid," he said. I didn't ask why both were swollen if he only slammed "it" in a door more than forty years ago. I again encouraged him to let us get him to a doctor, but he refused insisting he would be fine.

On the 7th, we saw him resting on the bench on Cañon again. As usual, he was smoking, but it was apparent he was too tired or winded to get to his office without stopping to rest. When we spoke with him later, his hands were not only swollen, one of them had been scraped on something sharp. Three wounds ran across the back of his left hand. Liz suspected they were self inflicted wounds from an attempt to relieve the pressure. I asked him again and he insisted he'd be fine.

"The swelling's from bugs that are living in my hands from the nuclear bombs they exploded a long time ago," he said with conviction. He didn't want to go to the doctor. The line between sane and crazy was again blurred in our minds. Liz's cancer had been linked to the nuclear tests done in the Nevada desert in the early sixties. Who were we to doubt the Mayor's belief?

By midmorning on the 8th we were becoming extremely worried. We went to check on Jeff. As we stood talking with him, a stranger suddenly threw himself between us and began frantically carrying on in a most confusing manner. At first, I thought we had another crazy guy, but as he wedged himself between us and the Mayor, he spoke with a voice near panic and dressed in an Irish accent, "Thank you for stopping. Thank you for stopping."

In the confusion, I didn't know if I should stand back and watch or try to protect Jeff by grabbing the man and throwing him aside.

"Don't mind him," stammered the stranger. He pointed at Jeff and said, "He just talks nonsense. Nothing he says makes any sense." I'd known the Mayor for many years and never showed as much disrespect as this man did in ten seconds of his mindless babbling. I'd be abusing understatement if I said he was starting to get on my nerves. I resisted the urge to be overly assertive and stood back and watched as the man identified himself as Reverend John of some obscure San Diego church. He began frantically saying, "We've got to get this man to a hospital. He's sick."

Liz tried to explain to the self appointed master of the Mayor that no one could force Jeff to go to the doctor against his wishes.

"Can't we call 911 or call the fire department?" he rambled.

"You can't make the man get into an ambulance if he doesn't want to go," explained Liz. Throughout the ordeal, the Mayor sat calmly watching and then he finally looked away and became invisible again. We thought the best thing we could do at that point was leave so we followed our shadows down Rosecrans.

A half hour later, we returned. The panicked preacher was nowhere to be seen. I asked the Mayor, "Is everything OK? Do you know that guy?"

He looked at me and after a pause said, "Oh, that guy that was here earlier? Yea, he's OK. He's from St. Agnes up the street." Jeff brushed him off almost as if he thought the reverend was a harmless crazy guy himself. I figured Jeff should know.

Although his spirits seemed to stay high, the week of the 9th passed with Jeff appearing to be increasingly tired. The swelling in his hands didn't diminish and he spent time lying on a bench across from his office. He could stretch out better than he could on his usual bench. Armrests partitioned it and made it impossible to actually lie down.

In the afternoon on Monday the 17th, I brought him something to eat, but he wasn't in his office. I spotted him lying on a flat bench across the street. When I went over there I found him sound asleep. I just left the meal on his duffel. The following morning he thanked us for bringing it by.

By the night of the 19th, he was too tired to get to his normal sleeping spot. He stayed on his bench all night. We had become intensely worried about him, but he continued to refuse any medical attention.

The next night, he spread his old sleeping bag on the hard, cold concrete directly in front of his bench. He slept there again the night of the 21st. He was tired and short winded, but he was still in good spirits, especially when considering the discomfort he was experiencing.

When we walked Saturday morning, Jeff had already put his sleeping bag away and was sitting in his normal place looking off into the southern sky. As he had done countless times in the past, he thanked us when we handed him a bag containing his favorite cheese bagel.

"Everything alright?" I asked, even though I knew it wasn't.

"Yea, I'll be OK," he said.

Liz and I were joining another couple that day at the Stone Brewing Company's annual beer festival in San Marcos. The Mayor was still studying the southern sky when we drove by. We came back to Point Loma around three in the afternoon. Everything seemed normal until I glanced toward the Mayor's office. It was empty.

"Oh, oh," I said. My remark needed no explanation. Liz's face reflected a grim, worrisome look. "I hope he's OK," I quietly said.

Twice more before the sun set, I walked down to look for the Mayor. He wasn't there. I hoped he had managed to find his way to his night refuge to rest. He was late arriving again Sunday morning. When he didn't show by noon, I went into the Village Store. Nabil "Bill" Goria, the owner, was behind the counter. "Where's Jeff?" I asked.

He seemed to stutter or choke a little as he tried to speak. Finally, in his heavy Iraqi accent as his eyes watered over, he said, "He's in heaven now."

Jeff had gone down just before noon Saturday. A doctor who happened to be nearby administered CPR as they waited for the ambulance. Neither the doctor nor the medical crew could revive our friend. The Mayor of Point Loma died in his office on Rosecrans Street.

Chapter Twelve
Meeting John Doe

Some things are most visible when they're absent. The Mayor's bench sat empty and there was a hole in our lives and in the fabric of Point Loma. Few things are truly constant, but Jeff was dependable, reliable and predictable. No matter what surprises the day would deal, we could always count on the Mayor. Who could have dreamed those many years ago when we first met him that Jeff would create such a gaping hole in our world when he was gone?

I felt compelled to make certain his case was being properly handled and that family had been notified. Without a last name, it was going to being difficult to get information, but I had to try my best for my old friend.

Engine Company 22 was the closest San Diego Fire Department location. It has been featured on national television shows because one of its crews is made up entirely of women. I was certain it would have been summoned to the Mayor's office. When I got to the fire station, a fresh crew had replaced the one that had worked the previous Saturday.

I explained the problem to the crew chief and he went directly to the log book. It took him just a few seconds to find what he was looking for. He explained, "They did respond to a 'man down' call Saturday the 22nd at 11:30 am. They were unable to revive the man. Finally, 'Medic 52' arrived and took him to UCSD Medical Center."

"Can you tell me his name?" I asked.

"We don't know it," he said. "The victim had no identification."

The next stop was the University of California San Diego Medical Center. But thanks to the "Health Insurance Portability and Accountability Act", HIPAA, getting health care information was going to be close to impossible even with a name. If the patient authorized the release of the information to me, no problem, but dead patients are rarely so cooperative. Immediate family members may be able to get around the rules, but I wasn't a blood relative. So with no last name, no relationship and the law stacked against me, I wasn't optimistic.

"I'm sorry, sir. Without a full name, I'm afraid there's really nothing I can do," explained a friendly, but too efficient hospital administrator. "If you can get a name, then maybe I can help you out."

I couldn't even get confirmation that the Mayor had died let alone information about whether or not his family had been notified. In my days as a mountain climber, the more difficult and challenging the mountain, the greater the determination required. I could see this was shaping up to be a tougher climb than I'd expected.

On my way home, I remembered the Mayor's explanation of why the "Teamster", another Point Loma homeless man, had invaded his space. The "Teamster" was trying to gain the ground of the Cabrillo students. Perhaps the Mayor was telling me he attended Cabrillo Elementary school when he was a boy. I went directly to the school.

I explained the situation to Patrice Wilson, the office manager, and asked if there were still copies of old yearbooks or class pictures. She said they were all locked up in the school library, but she would be happy to find them and turn me loose. I thought that if I could find a picture of a sixth grader that looked like the Mayor might have as a child, I could get the name from the picture.

Liz and I tried to guess the Mayor's age. After making allowances for the effects of sitting on a bench for years and subsisting on a diet of cigarettes and Winchell's donuts, we concluded he could be no younger than 48 and as old as 58. That meant if he had spent his sixth grade year at Cabrillo it would have been sometime between 1962 and 1973. The yearbooks were located and laid on a table in the library. I sat in a chair designed for the short legs of a sixth grader and began looking through the books. I started with the 1973 edition and worked my way backward in time.

When I opened the 1969 edition, the pages immediately looked different. It was then I discovered that prior to 1970, the names of the students were not printed below the pictures. If I were to be lucky enough to locate a picture that looked like the Mayor, the only way to identify the person would be if someone had manually written the student's name below the picture. This appeared to be the case with perhaps one in fifty pictures so the odds of finding the Mayor's name were close to zero.

After combing through yearbooks for nearly two hours, I found a picture that had enough similarities that I couldn't rule it out as a suspect. I made a photocopy. There was no name printed or written below. I searched Point Loma for someone that had graduated from Cabrillo in the year of the photo in hand. I found Bianca Romani and showed her the picture. Even though her picture was on the same page, try as she might, she could not remember the boy's name. She promised to contact others in her class to see if they could help. No one remembered the boy's name.

Later that day, I called a friend who works in law enforcement. After explaining the situation, I asked if there was an "insider's" way of getting the information. "I'll contact the coroner's office," I was told. "He's a very good friend of mine. I'm sure I can get a list of names of everyone that died that day." As it happened, the coroner was on vacation and wouldn't return for two weeks. It was another dead end.

A smarter person might have thrown in the towel, but I couldn't bear to let my friend down. I had to keep looking. I searched the internet for obituaries and death notices. This would become a daily ritual for the next few days. Surely at some point, someone would announce the passing of our Mayor. I looked for men in the appropriate age bracket that were named Jeff or David. None were found.

For many years, I'd written a weekly newspaper column in Arizona. I had also joined the throngs and taken the column into the blogosphere and published it as 54Candles.com. On the evening of August 25th, I sat down and wrote a piece entitled "Goodbye to a Dear Friend." The column summarized the history of my relationship with Jeff and bid him farewell. It seemed like the least I could do. Here is the opening paragraph and the closing paragraph of that column

> *Jeff died Saturday. He wasn't an average guy. For more than ten years, he sat on a bench at the corner of Rosecrans and Avenida de Portugal in the Point Loma area of San Diego. He was there for the millennium change. He sat there every Christmas morning. He rang in every New Year on the bench. Summers, winters, holidays, rain or shine, he was sitting on his bench. As you might imagine, he was different.*

> . . .

> *The Mayor died suddenly in his office last Saturday. His name was Jeff. Few people knew him. Many feared him. Others suffered his presence silently. We were delighted he invited us into his world. Like you and I, he was a singular point in the fabric of life we call humanity. He was our friend. And we're going to miss him terribly.*

Immediately, there was a spike in the level of readership of the blog. I watched over the next couple of days as readership seemed to be increasing exponentially. I was mystified as to why a piece about a man that had almost no friends and that spent most of his time in solitude was generating so much interest. The "Peninsula Beacon", a local newspaper dedicated to the beach communities of Point Loma and Ocean Beach printed the column and traffic increased still more.

I later learned that Pete Miller, a driver for FedEx who had driven by the Mayor for many years, had found the blog posting. He was moved by the story after long wondering about the mysterious man on the bench. Pete printed a copy of the column and pinned it on a bulletin board at the Postal Annex. He would also share the story with customers as he made his delivery rounds during the day. The story became a hot topic in Point Loma.

It was looking as if everyone had kept their own little secret from each other and now that the Mayor was gone, we were all looking at each other as if we had a sheepish confession to make. We all missed our crazy guy on the bench.

On the morning of Wednesday the 26th, we left for our morning walk with the Mayor's memory weighing heavily on our minds. As I walked out the door, I picked up an old flower vase and a handful of the fresh flowers we routinely kept around the house. As we came upon the bench, I placed the flowers on it and kept on walking.

Later that morning, we had occasion to walk past the bench and noticed the flowers were gone. We thought someone had seen them and concluded they'd been left for no reason and took them for themselves or for a sweetheart. We chuckled to ourselves.

The next morning, I again took fresh flowers to replace the ones borrowed the day before. Surely, the person who had taken them would now understand they hadn't been left there without reason and would leave them as a quiet remembrance of the man on the bench.

As we walked out the door Thursday morning we couldn't help but head directly to the Mayor's office. We were curious to see if someone had again used the flowers to claim the affection of his girlfriend. In the distance we could see the flowers still sitting there. As we got closer, we were surprised to see another bouquet of flowers on the bench. It warmed our hearts to find that someone else cared about our friend and had remembered him with flowers. There was no card or note.

Meanwhile, I was making little headway on my search for a name. In one way, I'd taken a step backward. I had finally received confirmation from the hospital that the Mayor had indeed died there. Sadly, he was "John Doe". He died without identification and as yet, no one on their staff had had any success in finding out who he was or whether or not he had any family. It saddened me to envision him lying on a cold metal shelf in the bowels of the hospital with a paper tag on a string tied to his toe naming him "John Doe". A woman in "decedent relations" at the hospital told me his case had been assigned to the county to seek name and family information. I called Bruce, the county employee in charge of the investigation. He had no information and said he was running out of time.

"What happens when you run out of time?" I asked.

With a tone of voice I'd expect from an executioner, he said, "We burn the body and dispose of the ashes at sea." My more pragmatic interpretation of his statement was, "It's dumpster time for the guy." I didn't want this happening to my friend.

Friday morning's walk brought more surprises. There was now a third and fourth flower grouping on the bench. The activity on the blog continued to climb and the comments started coming in. Saturday morning, more flowers appeared. To the back of the bench, someone had taped a note. It read:

> ### IN MEMORY OF THE MAN ON THE CORNER BENCH.
> *We will miss seeing you here daily!!! You became a "fixture" here, and we looked for you daily, and you were always here.....rain or shine. We know you are in a better place now....with the Angels.*
> *The Neighbors who walked this way.*

Other people cared about the crazy guy on the corner and that felt good.

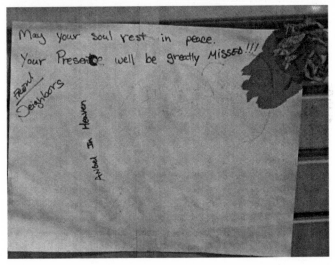

Chapter Thirteen
Revelations

Over the weekend more flowers and notes appeared on the bench. Some were from children. People began writing notes to Jeff as if he still sat there. Emotional confessions from strangers saying they had seen him sitting there for years, but had never stopped to say hello or help. They apologized for not letting the Mayor know they cared about him as a fellow human being and neighbor.

A call to the county case worker gave me a greater sense of urgency. If he couldn't find an identity and family by the end of the week, it was dumpsterville for the Mayor.

Blog activity went even higher than before. More and more comments came in, some with short accounts of experiences people had with the Mayor. They revealed the inner emotions of the writers and provided great insights into the personality of a schizophrenic whose life was centered on being invisible while sitting every day on a bench in the middle of Point Loma.

Flowers continued to fill the bench

One person told about taking his portable TV to the Mayor's office on the morning of September 11th, 2001 an hour after the first plane hit the World Trade Center. When the second plane hit, Jeff said, "It doesn't affect me." It hinted at how completely he tried to withdraw from the world.

Another writer posted a poem he'd seen on a tombstone.

> *The wonder of the world,*
> *The beauty and the power,*
> *The shapes of things,*
> *Their colours, lights and shades,*
> *These I saw.*
> *Look ye also while life lasts.*
> *R.I.P.*

I began to think I was witnessing a miracle of sorts. For years, I felt as if we were the only people that cared about a man whose life was dramatically different than the "normal" person's existence. Now I was watching as people's hearts started opening like the flowers of spring time. In a world filled with people too busy to say hello when passing on the street, the Mayor triggered a feeling of caring that usually lies hidden and dormant. The goodness of the heart was coming into bloom.

Finally, a post on the blog opened the door just a crack. Pete from FedEx had watched as the drama at the bench had rapidly intensified and he continued to share the story with others. He delivered some packages to Gary Trout, the owner of a private post office business named "Mail Call". Gary read the column and posted the following comment:

> *Jeff Pastorino.*
> *Many years ago I would accept his social security checks although that soon stopped. Jeff was a prolific writer of nonsense to the White House and the Treasury Dept. He would take out express envelopes from the UPS drop box across the street. In fact for a while he'd totally emptied the box! He would then address the envelopes and drop them in a Post office box. I finally had to hand him back about 50 letters and tell him to please stop or put some postage on. He lived in his own world and indeed, didn't bother people much. (Just the letters and yes, the Confederate dollar bills on occasion.) He could actually write quite well.*

I hoped this was the break I needed, but the race was far from finished. I began searching the internet for "Jeff Pastorino". I found absolutely nothing of significance. After many years, Gary Trout's memory may have faded a bit. Maybe the spelling was off. Maybe it was a name similar to Pastorino. Maybe it wasn't even close, but it's all I had. At least, it was all I had until I met Monica.

As the memorial continued to grow, it was common to see people standing at the bench reading the cards and notes with tears streaming down their faces. On one occasion, a woman stood reading the cards and letters. As I approached, she looked up and said, "He slept right behind my house." She told me there was a little known park area about a block from my house where she had seen the Mayor enter and sleep for years. I was amazed when I realized I'd walked the area for years myself and never noticed its existence.

That afternoon, I walked to the post office to pick up a package. As I passed the bench, a lone woman stared at the flowers. "Did you know him?" I asked.

"I was here when he died," she said. Her name was Monica and like so many Point Loma residents, she had seen the Mayor sitting on the bench for many years. After telling me more of the details of that fateful Saturday, she said a friend had assured her the Mayor's ex-wife lived just over the hill on the Ocean Beach side of the peninsula. She promised to call her friend and get the name.

Back home, a search of internet phone books and property records revealed no one named Pastorino living in the area. It was possible Jeff's ex-wife had remarried and taken a different name or maintained her maiden name. Then Monica called with a name and phone number. Maybe my search was over. My call reached an answering machine. I left my name and number. A couple hours passed and I hadn't received a return call. I left another message. Rather than wait for the return call, I used a reverse phone number search to get the address. Liz and I jumped in the car and drove to the house. Windows were open. The house was clearly lived in. We knocked on the door, but no one answered. We drove off.

An hour later, I was back knocking on the door. Still no one answered. As I turned to leave, a man approached from the side of the house. He said he was the home owner. When I told him who we were looking for he told us she had died a few years ago and he had purchased the house from the estate. As I pieced together the information he gave me, it became obvious I had gone down another blind alley.

As the sun fell toward the Pacific Ocean that Monday afternoon, I had reached a dead end on my internet search. I pondered my next step. I'd seen ads for companies that perform background checks, criminal investigations and other detailed searches on individuals, but they weren't cheap and there was no guarantee of success. I thought to myself, "What fool would be suckered into such a scheme?"

As I entered my credit card number, I answered my own question, fools like me. I had the report in a matter of minutes. I scanned the ten pages and it became obvious the reporting agency was shooting in the dark on a lot of the information. It looked like they took people with similar sounding names and hoped they might be relatives. They listed addresses associated with the person being investigated and enumerated neighbors at the same or adjacent addresses. It might have worked for people who lived in single family homes, but for someone picking up mail at a post office box, a listing of other box holders didn't offer much hope for insight. To make matters worse, I would learn that anything listed, past addresses, phone numbers or whatever, even if valid, may have been valid yesterday or twenty five years ago. I had a lot more to work with, but most of it amounted to false hopes and valueless leads. But the most promising piece of information appeared at the very top of the report. It read: Jeffrey Q. Pastorino, born July 11, 1957. It not only matched the name recalled by Gary Trout, it put his age right in the middle of the range we had guessed.

I could almost hear the band begin to play when I reached the bottom of page four. "Address 2: 2726 Shelter Island Drive, San Diego, CA 92106." This is the address of "Mail Call". I was now close to certain the Mayor was in fact Jeffrey Q. Pastorino. Now the challenge was to find his family before the investigator for San Diego County "disposed" of our friend.

I started working my way down the list of suspected relatives listed in the report. There were only four. Jerome Pastorino lived in Fort Lauderdale, Florida ten years ago. Another with the last name of Pas had a San Diego address in 2002. The remaining two were the most promising on the list. They appeared to be a husband and wife with the last name of Pastori. They were roughly a generation older than Jeff and could easily have been his parents. The address was reported as being very close to Point Loma and was just a year old. I could only guess as to why there was a slight difference in their last names from Jeff's, but after having done research on my own family, I knew name "shifts" were not uncommon. Even my own grandfather Radcliffe had adopted a last name that didn't match his father's, Ratcliff.

I called the phone numbers shown for the various parties. The Pas connection was the first to die. The phone had long been disconnected and there was no further sign of the person in the area. The phone tied to the Pastorino in Florida rang, but was never answered. I would keep trying, but after many attempts, hope faded.

The Pastori lead seemed to be the brightest, but it was also a tangled mess. Liz was working the phone as aggressively as I was and she finally made contact with the person living in the Pastori condo. After she explained the reason for the search, the woman told her she had purchased the unit from the Pastori's a year ago. She went on to say the Pastori's had moved into another unit on a different floor of the same building. We found it, contacted the owner and learned the Pastori's had moved into an assisted living center south of San Diego. The security office in the building confirmed this, but was unable to give us specifics as to where the Pastori's had gone. We called every assisted living center we could find in the south bay area. None of them had heard of any new residents named Pastori.

As the trail leading to the Pastori's grew more problematic, we continued to hunt for Jerome Pastorino in Fort Lauderdale. It didn't offer much hope; the address was ten years old and the phone was still not being answered. However, by this time we had learned "Pastorino" was not a very common name. We thought if we could locate Jerome Pastorino, he might be a distant relative and at least have some information of value.

As the clock continued to tick down in the county offices, we didn't have the luxury of waiting for people to return from vacations to return calls or for any more lucky breaks. I'd been a fool once. I doubled-down and purchased another background report, this time on Jerome D. Pastorino. I discovered he was two and a half years older than the Mayor. "A brother?" I wondered.

The report showed addresses in Hollywood, Pompano Beach, Davie and Miramar, Florida. It also showed addresses in Warminster, Pennsylvania. I guessed he wintered in Florida, but had his roots in Pennsylvania. Calls to the phone numbers listed in Warminster, like those made to Florida, went unanswered.

Unlike the report on the Mayor, this one had a substantial list of possible relatives, all with the last name Pastorino. As I scanned the list, Liz came into my office with some fresh information. She had been searching Warminster's public records for property ownership and discovered the address associated with Jerome in Warminster was actually owned by someone named Christopher Pastorino. If I could find Christopher, maybe he could lead me to Jerome who could maybe lead me to Jeffrey and maybe we could finally rest.

Try as we might, we couldn't find a home phone number for Christopher Pastorino. With more digging on the internet, I did stumble upon "Chris Pastorino Landscaping Company". I called. An answering machine told me to leave a message. I called again early Tuesday morning and left another message.

Around 9 am Tuesday morning as workers paused for lunch on the east coast, my phone rang. The voice on the other end said, "This is Chris Pastorino. You've been trying to get a hold of me?" I sensed a little wariness in his voice as if he was prepared to fend off a telemarketer.

"I'm trying to contact Jerome Pastorino," I said. "I thought you might be related." I suspected Chris might be a cousin or even Jerome's son.

"Jerry's my brother," Chris said. "Why are you trying to find him?"

I could barely contain my excitement. This was the first person I'd spoken to that might actually be a blood relative of the Mayor. It was apparent I was getting no more information from him without giving a more detailed explanation.

"I live in San Diego, California," I said. "A long time friend of mine named Jeff Pastorino passed away last week and I'm trying to locate his family. I'm thinking Jerome might be related."

I waited for a response, but all I heard was silence. "Are you there Mr. Pastorino?"

After more silence, a voice that sounded very different than it had minutes before hesitantly said, "He disappeared in 1982. I haven't seen him in twenty seven years. Jeffrey Pastorino is my twin brother."

The phone suddenly weighed twenty pounds. We shared silence for a few moments. I don't remember much about what was said after that. We both seemed shocked.

"I'll call you in the morning," he said. I think we hung up.

Chapter Fourteen

Homecoming

Chris Pastorino's brother, Jeffrey, afflicted with undiagnosed hebephrenic schizophrenia, walked out of the house one day in 1982 and vanished. Chris attempted to locate his brother, but failed at every turn. Now Chris sat in stunned silence parked in the driveway of a landscaping customer, his now silent cell phone in hand. His mind was rocked by turbulence every bit as brutal as that experienced by a small boat on the open ocean suddenly struck by an unexpected squall. Twenty-seven years of wonder, fear, doubt and worry battered him. He was paralyzed. He thought about starting his truck and leaving, but he could only huddle in the safe haven of the driveway as he tried to weather the storm. He was unable to move for over an hour.

When he finally drove home and shared the story with his wife and other family members, the protective shell that had been built over the past quarter of a century was shattered. When a brother disappears without a trace, it can be worse than if he had died. There is an absence, a hole in his world where the brother used to be. In that respect, it is no different from death. But unlike the death of a brother, there is no funeral, no closure and no finality.

The Pastorino family had to create a false sense of closure in the years after Jeff disappeared. But no matter how hard they tried, the unanswered questions always lurked in the shadows of their minds. Was Jeff alive? If so, where was he? Why can't they find him? Why can't or won't he find them? The questions weighed heavily on the family members, but to no one did they bring more torment than to the Mayor's twin brother.

Chris talked with his wife trying to organize his thoughts and feelings. He spent much of Tuesday night lying awake talking with the man in the mirror.

Wednesday morning dawned in San Diego. As soon as the County of San Diego offices opened, I was on the phone with the case worker responsible for locating the Mayor's family. We were within forty eight hours of disposal of Jeff's body.

"Have you located any family yet?" I asked.

The county employee said he had not and that he didn't have any leads. I got the impression that it might not be a shortage of leads that was hindering his investigation. It seemed more like motivation was in far shorter supply than were leads. He would be collecting his paycheck and Jeff would be just as dead regardless of the outcome of his search. I'm not sure what, if any, accountability there was in his section of the great bureaucracy we call government, but it struck me as odd that with his vast resources, he couldn't find the Mayor's family while a citizen armed with little more than a computer, a phone and a heart could do it.

I told him, "I'm pretty sure I've found the family. Please make sure nothing happens to Jeff until I get back with you." I didn't want to give him Chris' name and number until I'd talked directly with Chris and had his permission. There was still a chance, slim as it might be, that we had the wrong connection.

I spoke with Chris later that morning. He was still overwhelmed by what was happening, but was anxious to learn everything he could about what had transpired over the past twenty seven years with his brother. I told him about the situation with the county and gave him the name and number of the case worker. He said he would call.

Chris changed direction slightly and said, "I've been thinking a lot about this. I need to bring Jeffrey home to be buried next to our parents." His father died in January of the year Jeff disappeared. His mother died broken hearted nearly twenty years later. She lost her older son to the war in Vietnam in 1969. Although she didn't live long enough to discover why, she lost her youngest to mental illness in San Diego.

As all of this unfolded, the flowers of tribute, the notes and cards, votive candles and other remembrances continued to grow at and around the bench. When I told Chris about the growing memorial, he seemed to be touched and heartened to learn that so many people cared about his brother.

One of the more interesting cards left at the bench contained a heart rending, hand written note of farewell to Jeff. It was from a woman suffering from schizophrenia who has been on the streets of Point Loma for years. It was signed, "from Caroline, another person with a problem with brain chemistry." The remembrances were coming from people of all walks in life.

Chris called Friday and we had a lengthy discussion. He had made arrangements to have Jeff shipped back to Pennsylvania for burial. He had beaten the county deadline by less than twenty-four hours.

He asked what seemed to be an unending series of questions about Jeff. With twenty-seven years missing from their relationship, he was haunted by thoughts of what had happened. Who had his brother become? What was his life like? How and why did he come to San Diego? What did he talk about? Why did he live the way he did?

The discussion could have gone on indefinitely, but Chris finally paused and said, "You know, Howard, I feel like I've got to come to San Diego. I have to sit where he sat and see what he saw every day, the people, the buildings, the sights. I feel like it's the only way I can get to know him better."

He said he would check into flights and let me know when he would arrive. I offered to help him with whatever he needed.

Chris wasn't the only one with an endless list of questions. I finally had a way to learn about Jeff's early life. What drives a person to sit in one place for years and become invisible to the world around him? I knew Chris had a lot on his platter and was grieving so I didn't want to push the issue too hard. I knew there would be plenty of time later when he came to San Diego.

Chris and I communicated via email regularly and from time to time, we'd talk via phone. On the afternoon of October 6th, I received an email from Chris.

> *Jeffrey was finally laid to rest at 10:30 am today among family and old friends, it was a sunny 70 degrees just how Jeff liked it I imagined.*

I thought to myself, "We're getting close to the end of the story." I needed only to look at the growing memorial at the bench to realize we weren't even close. It had become common place to walk by the bench and see people standing there, reading, wiping wet eyes, neatening flowers and bowing their heads in prayer. Someone had taken a picture of the Mayor, put it in a frame and mounted it on the mesh behind the bench. I watched as a city bus made an unscheduled stop at the bench. The driver left her passengers sitting onboard with the engine running and approached the bench calling out, "Does anyone know what happened to the man on the bench?"

One morning as I was walking by I noticed a woman staring forlornly at the memorial. I asked her if she knew the man on the

People regularly stopped by the bench to read the cards and letters and leave flowers.
Photo courtesy of Larry Sheehan

bench. She looked up and didn't answer. When I suspected she may not speak English, I repeated my question in Spanish and the door opened. She explained she lived in Mexico, but had worked in Point Loma for many years. She had walked by the Mayor for years. "*Le extraño,*" she said with moist eyes.

A week later, Chris emailed me to say he would be arriving in San Diego November 5th to walk in the footsteps of his brother. He asked if I would post a note on the bench. He wanted everyone to know he was coming and hoped that anyone with any knowledge of Jeff would share that information with him directly. He wanted his phone number posted. He believed this was the only way he could get more insight into the brother he hadn't known for twenty-seven years. I promised him I would not only post the information, but that I would host an open house at my home when he came to San Diego. I would invite those with personal stories to come by my home and meet with Chris.

Now the memorial tribute at the bench took on more significance. I knew that with time, people would slowly stop bringing the flowers and letters. But for the sake of the Mayor's family, I hoped the tributes would continue at least until Chris came to San Diego. It seemed important to let him know that so many people cared. Who could have dreamed the Mayor could have touched the lives of so many people? I wanted Chris to know how important the Mayor had become.

One of the many notes left on the bench by children

By this time, people had found the email from Chris posted on the bench and they were beginning to send stories about the Mayor directly to Chris back in Pennsylvania. Some were calling him and sharing condolences and stories. Liz and I took it upon ourselves to maintain the bench area. As flowers died, we removed them. Any litter that appeared was promptly removed. If we were to keep it alive for three weeks, we had to keep it in top notch condition. All the while, little stories kept coming into the blog, the local newspaper website and to Chris personally. One small piece at a time, we were beginning to reconstruct the history of Jeffrey Pastorino, the Mayor of Point Loma.

Monday, October 12th was Columbus Day, a federal holiday. It was also a bank holiday. We went to the Mayor's office and removed any wilting flowers while we marveled at the new ones that had arrived. Someone had actually delivered a beautiful living plant with a touching personal note written to the Mayor. We walked away as the sun began its descent toward the Pacific horizon.

Chapter Fifteen
From the Jaws of Defeat

We walked our four miles the morning of Tuesday, the 13th. As we approached the Mayor's office, something looked amiss. As we walked closer, we realized the flowers were gone. The living plant, the emotional letters and cards, the candles and the framed photo were all gone. Even a small Bible that had been left by someone had been removed and thrown in the trash. We were stunned. How could anyone be so heartless as to destroy the loving memorial a community had put together in anticipation of the visit of the Mayor's twin brother?

Affixed to the framework of the Mayor's office is a brass plaque recognizing and thanking Union Bank of California for creating "this community plaza". We had always thought the plaque more than suggested the plaza was intended for the use of the "community". We didn't know who had removed the memorial, but we returned from our walk intent on finding out. We may have been the first residents of Point Loma to be outraged by this insensitive act, but we would soon find out we were far from the last.

As we walked the island that morning, we speculated as to who might have performed the dastardly act. Someone at the bank on the corner seemed to be the most likely suspect; the plaza was cut from a small corner of its parking lot. It was also the bank that had complained to the Peninsula Community Planning Board about the "growing problem of homeless people" on that corner. We kicked around the idea that various other people could have felt compelled to strip the corner of its decoration, but the prospect seemed farfetched at best. All we knew for certain was that sometime between four o'clock Monday afternoon and seven o'clock Tuesday morning, the memorial had been destroyed.

Within minutes of the bank's opening, I called to speak with the manager. I was told she wasn't available. After explaining I was a writer working on a "story", I was told she would return my call promptly. By the end of the business day, I was still waiting for the call.

The next morning I called right after the bank opened. I was again told the manager wasn't available. This time I didn't identify myself, but asked if the manager had a direct number. I wrote it down. Giving her the benefit of the doubt, I decided to await the return call from the previous day. By late afternoon, it hadn't come.

Shortly before the bank was to close, I called the private line of Sharon Jenkins, the branch manager. She immediately answered the phone. I identified myself and explained the reason for my call. I asked if she knew who had removed the memorial at the bench. She assured me she had no knowledge of the incident. In an attempt to divert the unwanted attention, she said, "Perhaps our landscapers took them."

Everything had disappeared between 4:00 pm on a bank holiday and 7 am the following morning. I knew, just as she did, the landscapers hadn't been there and they didn't dismantle the memorial, but I played along. I asked if she would share the phone number of the landscapers with me so I could ask. She was beginning to show more than minor annoyance, but gave me a number. It turned out she had sent me on the classic wild goose chase in the hopes that I would vanish.

I suggested that with such a massive outpouring of grief and community support the bank could end up with a bit of a black eye if it was in some way responsible. In a voice dripping with contempt she said, "Well, the bank does 'own' the property."

When I finally said, "The amount of warmth shown by so many members of the community has been far more than anyone had ever dreamed," she became haughty and caustic. With the compassion of Joseph Mengele, she remarked, "Well, I would think these people would be smarter if they spent their time helping someone that was still alive rather than someone that was dead?"

For the next few days, I tried to untangle the web of deception. Calls to the bank went unreturned. Those people I did get through to stonewalled my questions. All the while, the word on the street was spreading like a prairie fire that a bank employee driving a black car had destroyed the memorial late Monday.

Community members were outraged. The bank manager continued to deny having any knowledge of the act, but I found it interesting that she somehow discovered or divined it had taken place Monday afternoon when I had only said it took place between Monday afternoon and Tuesday morning. "It couldn't have been the bank," she later said. "It was Columbus Day and the bank was closed."

I guess she was suggesting bankers and black vehicles actually cease to exist on bank holidays.

Regardless of her level of involvement, two undeniable facts remained. The memorial had been destroyed shortly before the Mayor's twin brother arrived from Philadelphia and all of the tear stained mementos, pictures, cards and letters had been thrown away and forever withheld from family. With so little evidence of the existence of the Mayor for the past quarter century, a significant part of his legacy was taken forever. The people were outraged.

We vowed that with the memorial destroyed, we would plan a memorial event at the site. Chris Pastorino would arrive the evening of November 5th. Saturday the 7th would be event day in the Mayor's office. Mean spirited bank management was not going to stand in the way of a community's need to pay its respects to its long time friend.

If the event was to be a success, it needed to be publicized. For that, we needed something to publicize. It would be tough to convince people to come out and look at a long lost brother staring at an empty bench. There would need to be a brief, but meaningful service or presentation of some kind.

In San Diego, Father Joe Carroll is nearly legend. *Father Joe's Villages* (www.FatherJoesVillage.org) has provided food and shelter for the homeless and poor for more than a half century. He serves more than 3,000 meals every day to those who would otherwise go hungry. To San Diegans, Father Joe is an amalgamation of Mother Teresa, Gandhi and Elvis. If someone has lived in San Diego for more than 60 minutes, they've heard of Father Joe.

If we could get Father Joe to conduct the memorial, it would be a coup of the highest order. It would draw media attention, community participation and show great respect not only for the Mayor, but other homeless, mentally ill people with similar life stories. Unfortunately, with his celebrity status, Father Joe was a commodity in great demand and short supply. We wondered if we would stand a better chance going after Elvis, but nothing ventured, nothing gained.

I called the headquarters of Father Joe's Villages and was referred to Jopo Valera, the head of marketing and media relations. He agreed to meet with us Monday afternoon.

On Saturday the 17th, I received an email from someone named Ann Campbell. She was understandably confused. The subject line read "Are you the Howard Jones?", but the body of the message was addressed to "Allen".

> *Dear Allen,*
>
> *I read an article by Howard Jones about Jeff Pastorino. Chris, Jeff's brother, told me Howard Jones had an "Allen" in his name...would that be you? I understand that Chris is coming out to meet people who might know something about his brother and that you might be having an open house. If I have the right person, please let me know. I would like to help in some way.*

All the best,
Ann
(from Point Loma)

For many years, my newspaper column had been written under the pen name "Allen Sherpa". However, when the *Peninsula Beacon* published my piece on the homeless man of Point Loma, the byline read "Howard Jones". The result with Ann, Chris and others was a touch confusing. The signature graphic at the bottom of her message caught my eye, "Director of Strategic Planning – San Diego Opera". And she wanted to help with an "open house". Ann had experience dealing with those who frequent the highest echelon of "society" and she wanted to help. I instantly thought the chances of success for the memorial service had just shot skyward. We agreed to meet at a local coffee shop the following Tuesday afternoon.

On Monday, Liz and I snaked our way through an industrial area in south San Diego and finally found the main offices of Father Joe's Villages. As we waited in the reception area, we picked up a newspaper and found the picture of Dr. David Folsom, a noted community oriented psychiatrist. He had just been appointed the Medical Director for Father Joe's Villages. A couple of years before, we had enjoyed dinner with Dr. Folsom as we questioned him about the Mayor and other mentally ill homeless people and the things that run through their minds.

Jopo Valera was gracious and welcoming. He seemed to be moved by the story of Mayor Jeff Pastorino and promised to pitch the idea to Father Joe. However, he encouraged us not to be overly optimistic. "Father Joe's schedule is very full and he usually can't break free unless it's for a larger group," he said. We left with some hope, but were thinking we needed to work on "Plan B".

Tuesday afternoon, we met with Ann Campbell. She conveyed an image of unmitigated class and radiated warmth with her captivating smile and welcoming personality. I explained the dual personality issue between Allen Sherpa and Howard Jones. She said she lived in the neighborhood and for years had driven by the Mayor, but had never paused to talk with him. She stopped at the flower bedecked bench and read the cards and letters. She was overwhelmed with grief, sadness and regret for never having offered a hand to the Mayor. She took Chris Pastorino's number and tearfully called him and apologized for her lack of action over the years.

Chris told her of my promise of an open house and she wanted to square the ledger by helping in whatever way she could. She said her schedule was very demanding with the opera at that time, but she wanted to help in some way even if it was only to contribute money to a fund. I assured her the offer was much appreciated and that I was certain she could be of assistance. I then told her what had happened with the flowers, cards and tributes at the bench. She was stunned. I told her about my plans for a memorial service at the bench. She was delighted with the idea and all but begged to help.

"Why don't you call Father Joe?" she said. "He has dedicated his life to helping the homeless and less fortunate."

"Funny you should bring that up," I said. "I met with his media relations guy just yesterday. He's going to try and get Father Joe to do the event."

Her first major contribution to the event came as a surprise. "He's a friend of mine," she said. "Do you want me to call him?" I tried to restrain my answer thinking it was inappropriate to bellow, "Hell yes. Are you joking?" to someone I had just met. "That would be great," I said.

We talked at some length about the memorial service. As a tactful person who gets along everywhere she goes, Ann felt we should get "permission" from the bank to hold the service in the Mayor's office. I was more inclined to have it without consent. If they could deal with the potential public relations nightmare of hauling Father Joe and a group of mourners off in a paddy wagon then fun would be had by all. But in a spirit of cooperation and compromise, I acquiesced, especially after she said, "I know the regional manager and I'll give him a call. He's a real nice man. It shouldn't be a problem."

"It shouldn't have been a problem to leave the flowers on the bench until Chris' arrival," I whispered to myself.

When we returned to the house, Liz disappeared into her office and busied herself on the computer. On a hunch, she searched the county property records and discovered that despite the bank manager's claim that "we own the property," the bank was only leasing it. Liz came into my office and said, "The property is actually owned by Nancy Peckham, the widow of Peter Peckham, the man whose name is engraved on a brass plaque on the bench." Peter and Nancy Peckham have been some of San Diego's great philanthropists and benefactors with heavy involvement in the San Diego Zoo, the Navy League, Rady Children's Hospital and the rejuvenation of San Diego's spectacular downtown area. They used to be owners of the San Diego Padres baseball team. Liz called Nancy and found she was a friendly, warm and welcoming person. Nancy told about how she and Peter used to drive past the Mayor and smile. "Look," she would say. "The man is still using your bench." They would smile about their contribution to the well being of the crazy guy on the corner. She was saddened by his death and outraged at the dismantling of the memorial that had been assembled on her bench.

Meanwhile, the comments and letters to the editor continued to pile up on the blog and at the Peninsula Beacon. More and more stories about the Mayor's life were being brought to the fore.

I learned Jeff Pastorino had arrived in Point Loma nearly eighteen years before. The "community plaza" didn't yet exist and he sat on a nearby bench on Shelter Island. He wore a three-piece suit. He wore the suit every day, the same suit. Some people concluded he was an attorney. Others said he was an accountant. He never drank alcohol, never took drugs. The suit became increasingly weathered and after a year or so started falling apart. Someone living aboard a sailboat in the marina took his old foul weather gear, a hooded coat and pants, cleaned it up and gave it to Jeff. This was to become his wardrobe style for nearly two decades.

We discovered the Mayor's living expenses had been secretly covered by various members of the community. A local architect would go into the Village Store and put fifty or a hundred dollars on account to cover the Mayor's cigarettes and snack needs. Another person would give money to Gus' Pizza to pay for his sandwiches. Some people would, from time to time, slip him a ten or twenty dollar bill. It seemed the man who never asked for a thing never had a need. People were silently and secretly helping other people.

Some of the stories told a great deal about the man and his illness. As I had learned as his friend, he had a great interest in financial matters. Mayla Woo from the Cañon Street Coin Laundry, a block from the Mayor's office, told a story of being an unwilling observer to one of his more creative financial transactions. She watched ten years before he died as he attempted to purchase a house in Point Loma. Mayla crossed the parking lot separating her business from Point Loma Drugs to make a copy of a document. The Mayor had just arrived to use the machine and Mayla watched as he took money from his jacket pocket. He laid as many one hundred dollar bills as would fit on the copier surface and started feeding the machine with coins. It soon became apparent his intention was to use the machine to make many copies. Mayla asked him if he would allow her to make just one copy before he finished. He declined and continued producing copy after copy of his hundred dollar bills. Mayla stood by and watched. She finally got her chance, made her copy and returned to the laundry.

Mayla watched through the window as the Mayor walked her way, removed a plastic chair from the laundry and placed it on the sidewalk. He sat down, produced a pair of scissors and began cutting out the copies of the bills. This went on for about an hour. When he had finished trimming the last bill, he had a stack of hundreds perhaps six inches high. He took a real estate company's "Homes" magazine and removed the page highlighting the house he wished to buy. He wrapped the bills in the page, placed everything in a large manila envelope, sealed it and walked down the street to the real estate office which had long since closed for the day. He placed the envelope in the night drop and returned to his office. I doubt the deal was ever consummated and Mayla didn't know if the Mayor's payment was ever refunded.

It was around the same time the Mayor's life suffered a substantial disruption. The old retail building that had long stood at the corner of Rosecrans and Avenida de Portugal was to be torn down and replaced with the new bank building and parking lot. During the construction period, his bench wasn't available. He spent his days sitting on some steps behind the construction site all the while watching as the face of his immediate world was being changed. After the construction had finally been completed and the "community plaza" dedicated, he moved to his new bench in his old location. If his home purchase had gone through, maybe he wouldn't have had to endure such inconvenience.

Housed in the little strip-center where the Mayor sat watching the construction is a deli run by a lady from Thailand. One day, one of her ovens stopped working properly. The Mayor got wind of the problem and took it upon himself to help out. He began writing a set of instructions on how to resolve the mechanical problem and get her back in business. He took the four pages of detailed corrective actions to the deli owner. She thanked him and he left. As she read, the written instructions were clear and logical for at least one or two lines. Then they "hebephrenically" began to wander. By the time she was done, it wasn't clear they had anything to do with ovens, baking, delis or Point Loma. But with a good heart and the best of intentions, the Mayor had stepped forward to assist.

Over the years, he had taken small, not always wise, but always well intended, steps to help people. Slowly, the neighbors grew to accept the crazy guy on the bench as one of their own. Maybe that's why good hearted people like Ann Campbell felt so bad when their last chance to help their neighbor was buried in Pennsylvania.

I received two calls from Ann that Monday. The first was to announce she had spoken with Father Joe and he had committed to performing the memorial service November 7th. I was elated. She was delighted and proud as she should have been.

Banner announcing memorial service for the Man on the Bench

The second call came that evening. There was no joy in her voice, only shock. She had talked with the bank's regional manager about getting permission to hold the memorial service at the community plaza. She had not only been told we couldn't do so, she was subjected to a hateful rant about how Jeff was a disgusting bit of humanity. He would have no part of doing anything that would honor or perpetuate his memory. When she reported this to me, she was shaken and near tears. "I've never seen this man behave this way or talk with hate and anger," she said. "It was totally out of character."

Ann started proposing alternative locations. "Maybe we can hold it right across the street in the parking lot at the Village Store," she suggested.

I waited for her to exhaust her alternatives and then I suggested (without alternative) we would hold it in the Mayor's office right where he sat every day of the year. "If the bank has control of the 'community plaza,' they certainly don't own the public sidewalk and right-of-way," I said. "Assuming they have the legal right to rope off the plaza itself, I'll be delighted to help them. I'll also be delighted to make the signs we'll hang on the ropes explaining why the citizens of Point Loma were being kept out."

We moved forward with the plan. The following day, like Merlin the Magician, Ann pulled another rabbit from her hat. (Yes, I know – Merlin didn't do the rabbit from the hat trick. Please don't ask for your money back.)

Ann said, "A neighbor and friend of mine is the president of one of the biggest public relations firms in San Diego. Do you mind if I talk with her about this?"

It was another "you must be joking" moment, but I again rose to the challenge and responded almost casually. "No, that'll be great," I said. Karen Hutchens is President of Hutchens PR. It's her job to be well connected and she does it well. We were trying to get publicity for the November 7th memorial and to draw attention to Mayor Pastorino and the plight of the mentally ill homeless population in general.

When Karen learned about the homeless man who had become the focal point for so many different people in Point Loma she saw a very compelling story. As luck would have it, Karen had a lunch date with Karin Winner the following day. Winner was the Editor of The San Diego Union-Tribune, the major newspaper in the San Diego area with a circulation of approximately 400,000. At lunch, they talked about the Mayor. Karin Winner was overwhelmed. She said she'd assign her best writer to the story.

Veteran writer, John Wilkens wasted no time. He asked if he could meet with us as soon as possible. We invited him to the house. He had already done a lot of homework by the time he arrived. He'd spoken with Chris Pastorino and a couple of other people. We talked about the Mayor and our experiences with him for nearly two hours. He was very thorough and professional. The story was scheduled for the Sunday edition. This would be absolutely perfect timing for the memorial six days later. When he left, we crossed our fingers and hoped for the best. I anticipated a nice little human interest story buried somewhere in "Section D" of the paper. I don't know what percentage of the 400,000 readers would stumble into that section of the paper, but any publicity would be good publicity.

Wilkens called Thursday the 29th to ask if we could meet one of the Tribune's photographers at the bench the following morning. He suggested I bring a picture of the Mayor that I'd had framed for Chris Pastorino's visit. When I arrived at the bench, the photographer was setting up enough equipment to open a photo studio and people were turning their heads trying to figure out what was going on. He took lots of shots as we talked about a major news story that was just breaking. A U.S. Coast Guard transport plane searching for some missing boaters had just collided with a U.S. Marine helicopter somewhere off the coast of San Diego. There were numerous fatalities and people were missing at sea. The photographer said most staff writers had been pulled from whatever tasks they had been working on to cover the military rescue operations. He said there was a good chance John Wilkens would not be able to complete the story by his deadline. Unfortunately, the world's events didn't always occur at convenient times.

The spectacle of setting up a photography shoot on a street corner had drawn some spectators. As I started to walk away, a man approached and introduced himself as Dan Patel. He owned the motel directly across the street. He was there the day the Mayor died.

We talked for a while about our experiences with Jeff. Dan said he always tried to keep an eye on him and felt he was a part of the neighborhood. Dan mentioned the police had asked him if he could hold on to the Mayor's duffel bag. After two months, no one had called or asked for it. I told him I was in regular contact with the Mayor's brother Chris and that I'd be happy to take the bag from him, go through it and let his brother know what I found. Although this was true, I didn't tell him how my curiosity raged with a desire to know if any of the Mayor's writing was in the bag. I thought about all the times I'd told him he should write about the stories he told. I would love to see the written accounts if they existed.

I got to the house with the duffel over my shoulder. It had an "air" about it. I left it in the garage. I told Liz what I had and she accompanied me back into the garage. Even with the back door and the double garage door open to give us some air movement, Liz decided I should inventory the bag while she waited inside the house where the air was less like an anaerobic swamp sample on a hot summer night.

I pulled out his sleeping bag. It wasn't a pretty sight, but it looked better than it smelled. In my mountain climbing days after weeks at altitude with no running water I probably had some things in the same league, but it was cold and odors were quickly whisked away by the icy mountain winds. The bag went directly into the trash can and the lid was quickly closed. Out came the Mayor's extra pair of boots, a pair of pants, his shaving kit and some underclothes. They followed the sleeping bag into the trash. Out came his fork, spoon and knife, a couple of batteries and a little "Walkman" someone had probably given him. It appeared to have never been used. As I removed items from the bag, dozens of plastic fork tynes came with everything. He had obviously tried to save plastic forks over the years only to have them break while they were in the duffel. The last item of any bulk came out. A large plastic Ziploc bag with coins and other metal objects. I opened the bag and saw thirty or forty coins. Most of them were foreign. Some were Mexican pesos issued before the devaluation of the peso many years before; they were all but worthless. There were tokens for games at a local pizza parlor and some good luck coins. He had collected lead weights used to balance tires and saved them along with the coins. It was an interesting collection of things, but to estimate the total value of the contents of the bag at fifty cents would probably be overly optimistic.

The duffel felt empty as I opened it wider. There on the bottom of the bag was what I had been seeking, writings from the Mayor. There weren't many, but I reached in and removed them. As I did, the tines of plastics forks fell onto the garage floor. Clipped to the papers was a colorful pen that had come from Windsor Castle near London, England.

I was excited to hold some of the last private writings of the Mayor in my hand, but as I read through them, I was saddened to learn that none of them were written to describe some of the bizarre realities we had shared together and that I had encouraged him to commit to paper. That's not to say they weren't interesting. They definitely were full of insights as to what runs through the mind of a schizophrenic like the Mayor.

In his mind, he was the president of a company named *Investment Group Banker, Inc.* He appears to have spent much of his time coming up with investment ideas and business plans. In one instance he proposed a plan whereby quantities of Robert Rothchild Buffalo Bleu Cheese Dip could be purchased at Baron's Market Place and made into salad dressing and ultimately melted onto hot dogs, macarone n' cheese [sic]. Rothchild would support the product and the proceeds from sales would be used for school education. Advertising would be through "City Beat" newspapers and would be the responsibility of Union Bank of California with whom he was partnering in the venture. His proposal was signed "Jeffrey Querino Pastorino".

One of the more complex plans called for a joint venture with Prudential California Realty Association and the meat industry to work with the provisions of some "1918 act" to issue new currency he called the "Lewis n' Clark" dollars. They would be printed in $10,000, $100,000 and $1,000,000 denominations.

As with his conversations, his business plans tended to begin with focus and quickly roll off and over the hill into a difficult to follow collection of almost random thoughts. One missive written under the "Investment Group Banker" heading gave some insight into his sense of right and wrong. He found two pennies near his office and must have assumed they belonged to the bank. He wrote the following note to Union Bank of California:

> *Enclosed two damage pennies of coins in dental drill, founds by Canon St. Tar damage from street.*

It also highlighted his constant preoccupation with the medical profession. In his life, damage was almost always the result of something or someone in the medical profession.

The bag of coins and lead tire weights, the Mayor's written words and his pen from the Queen of England were put in a box. They would be the sole physical mementos Chris would have from the past twenty-seven years of his brother's life.

Sunday morning we were four days from Chris' arrival in San Diego and six days away from the memorial service. As we left for our morning walk, we talked about our plan to distribute flyers to local businesses in the hope of getting a good turnout at the memorial. After losing the entire collection of letters and cards to the stone cold heart of someone, we wanted to at least have enough people turn out to let Chris know there were people that cared about his twin. By now we had learned that we weren't the only people that cared, but we feared not many others would want to sacrifice a half hour in the middle of their Saturday to honor a crazy guy on a bench. If we could even get a dozen people to attend, we would feel like we'd been successful, especially now that the big news story had no doubt pushed us out of this week's Union-Tribune. After all, as the bank manager had so warmly stated, most people might think it's a waste to spend all this time and effort on some crazy dead guy.

As we rounded the corner on Rosecrans, we walked by a vending machine for the San Diego Union-Tribute. As we expected, at the top of a big two column story was the block headline "Hope fading in crash of military craft." Then we froze in our tracks. There, staring through the glass of the door and taking the rest of the front page was a large, color photograph of

The front page of The San Diego Union-Tribune the Sunday before the Jeff Pastorino memorial

me holding the picture of the Mayor. It was the headline story of the entire Sunday edition, three columns, big picture and a headline that simply said "Man on the Bench." The writer led the story with a secondary headline of "The community that took care of a homeless man mourns his death – and finds his long-lost twin brother." There were more pictures, maps and a marvelous history. We couldn't have asked for greater publicity. The story was face to face with everyone in California south of Los Angeles that morning. We were elated.

By the end of the day Monday, three large, eye-catching banners announcing the event had been hung in the village compliments of Ann Campbell, the woman with a heart of gold. One hung over the Mayor's bench with the permission of the bank. Apparently someone had started to realize it was time to stem the bleeding from a public relations wound. Vons grocery store in Liberty Station generously promised lots of flowers for the Saturday morning of the service. Flyers were distributed to area businesses and more stories about the Mayor's past started pouring in.

Now it was a matter of making sure all the last minute arrangements were being handled. Father Joe's arrival time was confirmed. We also had to deal with our own last minute worries. If Jeff Pastorino had a mental illness that is known to run in families, what if Chris Pastorino was just as crazy and wasn't even truly coming? Maybe he was locked up in an institution. Maybe he wasn't even the Mayor's brother. Oh my! What if we're the crazy ones after all?

Chapter Sixteen
Touching the Void

It was nearly ten o'clock at night when Chris Pastorino called. "I've checked in at the Cabrillo Inn across from the bench. I feel like I've got to walk over to the bench just to be where Jeffrey spent all those years. I'll give you a call in the morning."

"If you need anything, just give us a call," I said. "We walk every morning. If you're up and feel like walking, keep an eye out for us around six."

Thursday morning was a little brisk. Fall was in the air. As we walked toward the bench, we saw a thin, dark haired man quietly standing there. "Hello, Chris," I said.

"Hi," he responded. For the first time since the adventure began, I was certain we had the right person. Chris was much thinner than his brother, but as I looked into his eyes, I saw the Mayor's eyes. When I looked at his mouth, I saw the Mayor's lips.

Chris couldn't contain his curiosity. He launched a barrage of questions about his brother. "Where did he sit? Where did he sleep? What did he wear? What time was he here? Did he ever talk about his family?" We did

Chris Pastorino mourns at the bench

our best to answer his questions, but finally said we were going to walk and asked him if he'd like to join us. "We can talk as we walk,"

I said. As it turned out, he would join us for our morning walk every day he was in San Diego.

We had our questions too. "What kind of a kid was he growing up? What were his hobbies? How was he socially? In school?" The questions were endless on both sides. It seemed as if there was so much information being passed back and forth, someone could have written a book. When we'd completed the walk, Chris came back to the house and Liz put together one of her gourmet breakfasts. After another hour of talk, we parted ways. We agreed to get back together before lunch for a "walking tour" of the Mayor's domain.

We met again before lunch and I led Chris on a tour of the Mayor's world. I took him to where he spent his nights, the stores he frequented and the paths he walked. I tried to introduce him to the people with whom Jeff regularly came in contact. Emotions ran high. Strangers embraced Chris and shared their condolences with him. They told him little stories about his brother and assured him that the Mayor may have been a little different, but he was our neighbor and friend.

When I took Chris into the Village Store, the owner was working the counter. Bill was raised in Iraq, but had immigrated to this country and bought his store not long before the Mayor himself arrived in Point Loma. Bill saw the Mayor every day. Bill was the source of his cigarettes and much of his food. Bill welcomed Chris with open arms and they talked of Jeff. At some point, the discussion found its way to the subject of people helping others like the Mayor. The emotion began building in Bill's voice and his eyes became moist. "It isn't right," he said as his voice rose. "We can spend millions of

Nabil N. Goria, the owner of the Village Store in Point Loma dollars for bombs to kill innocent people, but we can't help a poor man like Jeff."

We moved on to Shelter Island Drugs. The staff greeted Chris like family. Then on to the laundry where Chris was hugged by a teary eyed Mayla Woo. It was like this for the entire walk. Chris' emotions were thrown around like tissue in a tornado. Everywhere he went he felt the love the community had for his brother. When we finally got back to the house, he was emotionally exhausted.

Over lunch, we talked about their years growing up in Pennsylvania. Chris and Jeffrey couldn't have been much more non-identical twins. Jeff was a social butterfly more interested in having a good time than cracking the books. Chris was more studious and loved baseball. Chris and I shared a love of the game.

The Pastorino family lived outside Philadelphia and as far as Chris was concerned, there was no other team than the Phillies. He had season tickets and had attended game four of the World Series just four days before. His Phillies had lost to the New York Yankees. The boys of summer had finished their season less than thirty six hours before we sat down for lunch. The Phillies were defeated in game six, but that didn't diminish Chris' loyalty to the team. "Next year," he said.

We didn't see each other the rest of the day. I had a couple of commitments I had to honor and Chris wanted to go to the hospital and the San Diego County offices to learn as much about the Mayor's death as possible. The next time we would meet would be at the memorial Saturday at noon. Hopefully we wouldn't be the only ones there. I was still hoping for as many as a couple dozen people, but I wondered what would happen if more showed up. As a precaution, I found a company on the other side of San Diego that specialized in providing equipment for rock bands. I rented a speaker and remote microphone. I suspected a sound system was overkill, but better safe than sorry.

Friday night's sleep was a restless one with dreams of the bank having the only five people present arrested and hauled off to the calaboose. The weather was supposed to be a little cool by San Diego standards and I suspected that if it was to ever snow in paradise, Saturday would be the day. As I watched the sun sink slowly into the ocean Friday evening, the sky glowed red. I could only hope old sailors were right.

I was up well before dawn. After our morning walk, I drove to VONS to pick up the flowers. I was delighted to discover they'd put aside enough flowers to fill my car. An employee helped haul bouquet after bouquet to the parking lot. I stopped at the bench and was surprised and pleased to find other flowers had already been delivered. I was home by nine and had nothing to do but wait and worry.

By eleven, I could wait no more. I convinced myself it could take as much as an hour to setup the sound system. I loaded up the car and headed toward the Mayor's office. There were already a couple dozen people milling about. Chris was there. Members of the media were there. By the time I was done setting up the sound system, the crowd had grown to fifty or sixty people. People lined up to meet Chris. Others greeted each other with embraces. It was obvious my fears of no one caring enough to pay last respects to the crazy guy on the bench were overly pessimistic.

When Father Joe Carroll arrived at quarter to twelve, the crowd had grown to 150 people. Father Joe exuded a sense of calm and humility. His disarming smile brightened the day for every one there. He graciously greeted the many mourners that lined up to meet him.

As people continued to arrive, I watched as a homeless man I'd seen in the area many times before approached the Mayor's bench. He was disheveled, soiled and unshaven, much as he had been the other times I'd seen him. He stood before the massive pile of flowers with his head hung low. Tears washed away the dirt on his cheeks. He offered a quiet prayer to the Mayor. When he slowly raised his head, turned and began to walk away, he spotted me standing in the background. He walked directly toward me, stopped, reached out and hugged me. He had a distinct odor of alcohol and in his tired, weathered face, he had the look of a damaged, flawed and lost human being. But it was almost as if he had a twinge of hope. Someone cared about the Mayor. Maybe someone could care about him.

The crowd gathers at the bench to pay its respects to Jeff Pastorino

With ten minutes to go I was stunned as I scanned the crowd and saw the amazing cross section of people of Point Loma that came to say goodbye to their friend. It was then that another mystery was solved.

In the years I knew the Mayor, regardless of the weather, he always wore a weather resistant, hooded coat not unlike those worn by sailors and mountain climbers. But every few months, he would get a new one along with a new pair of hiking style boots. Liz and I would debate the source of his new clothes. I argued that a commercial fisherman washed a well worn coat and gave it to the Mayor. Liz cautioned me, "Never argue with a woman over fashion. That's a brand new coat."

Liz was right. The man that bought the new coats for the Mayor arrived. Even though baseball's World Series had just ended, one of the game's great second basemen cut short his stay in Philadelphia to fly back for the memorial. Los Angeles Dodgers great Davey Lopes was another friend of the Mayor that chose to remain anonymous. He maintained his off-season home in Point Loma and when he was in town, he would buy an extra breakfast at the nearby deli and take it to the Mayor. One of the game's all time great base stealers and a major league manager and coach, Lopes had credentials matched by a select few in the history of the game. His heart was as big as his bat. He took care of his friends and Mayor Jeff Pastorino was one of those lucky people. Less than a week before, Chris Pastorino had watched from the stands as Lopes stood in front of him

Dodger great Davey Lopes talks with Chris Pastorino

coaching the Phillies in the World Series. Now they shared their grief in the Mayor's office.

As I scanned the crowd, I saw a "Who's Who of San Diego". Nancy Peckham, a former owner of the San Diego Padres professional baseball team and one of San Diego's great benefactors looked on. Sharon Zell (Brown), a former Miss USA came to pay her respects to the Mayor. One of the originators of the Tommy Bahama brand of clothing was present. San Diego artists and entertainers were there. Merchants, business owners, community leaders, princes and paupers washed the sidewalk with their tears as Father Joe told the story of the The Little Prince and how he tamed the fox.

It was then that the fox appeared.

"Good morning," said the fox.

"Good morning," the little prince responded politely, although when he turned around he saw nothing.

"I am right here," the voice said, "under the apple tree."

"Who are you?" asked the little prince, and added, "You are very pretty to look at."

"I am a fox," the fox said.

"Come and play with me," proposed the little prince. "I am so unhappy."

"I cannot play with you," the fox said. "I am not tamed."

"Ah! Please excuse me," said the little prince.

But after some thought, he added:

"What does that mean – 'tame'?"

"You do not live here," said the fox. "What is it that you are looking for?"

"I am looking for men," said the little prince. "What does that mean – 'tame'?"

"Men," said the fox. "They have guns, and they hunt. It is very disturbing. They also raise chickens. These are their only interests. Are you looking for chickens?"

"No," said the little prince. "I am looking for friends. What does that mean – 'tame'?"

"It is an act too often neglected," said the fox. "It means to establish ties."

"To establish ties?"

"Just that," said the fox. "To me, you are still nothing more than a little boy who is just like a hundred thousand other little boys. And I have no need of you. And you, on your part, have no need of me. To you, I am nothing more than a fox like a hundred thousand other foxes. But if you tame me, then we shall need each other. To me, you will be unique in all the world. To you, I shall be unique in all the world . . ."

"I am beginning to understand," said the little prince. "There is a flower . . . I think that she has tamed me."

"It is possible," said the fox. "On the Earth one sees all sorts of things."

"Oh, but this is not on the Earth!" said the little prince.

The fox seemed perplexed, and very curious.

"On another planet?"

"Yes."

"Are there hunters on that planet?"

"No."

"Ah, that is interesting! Are there chickens?"

"No."

"Nothing is perfect," sighed the fox.

But he came back to his idea.

"My life is very monotonous," the fox said. "I hunt chickens; men hunt me. All the chickens are just alike, and all the men are just alike. And, in consequence, I am a little bored. But if you tame me, it will be as if the sun came to shine on my life. I shall know the sound of a step that will be different from all the others. Other steps send me hurrying back underneath the ground. Yours will call me, like music, out of my burrow. And then look; you see the grain-fields down yonder? I do not eat bread. Wheat is of no use to me. The wheat fields have nothing to say to me. And that is sad. But you have hair that is the color of gold. Think of how wonderful that will be when you have tamed me! The grain, which is also golden, will bring me back the thought of you. And I shall love to listen to the wind in the wheat . . ."

The fox gazed at the little prince, for a long time.

"Please – tame me!" he said.

"I want to, very much," the little prince replied. "But I have not much time. I have friends to discover, and a great many things to understand."

"One only understands the things that one tames," said the fox. "Men have no more time to understand anything. They buy things all ready made at the shops. But there is no shop anywhere where one can buy friendship, and so men have no friends any more. If you want a friend, tame me . . ."

"What must I do to tame you?" asked the little prince.

"You must be very patient," replied the fox. "First you will sit down at a little distance from me – like that – in the grass. I shall look at you out of the corner of my eye, and you will say nothing. Words are

the source of misunderstandings. But you will sit a little closer to me, every day . . ."

The next day, the little prince came back.

"It would have been better to come back at the same hour," said the fox. "If, for example, you come at four o'clock in the afternoon, then at three o'clock I shall begin to be happy. I shall feel happier and happier as the hour advances. At four o'clock, I shall already be worrying and jumping about. I shall show you how happy I am! But if you come at just any time, I shall never know at what hour my heart is to be ready to greet you . . . One must observe the proper rites . . ."

"What is a rite?" asked the little prince.
"Those also are actions too often neglected," said the fox. "They are what make one day different from other days, one hour from other hours. There is a rite, for example, among my hunters. Every Thursday they dance with the village girls. So Thursday is a wonderful day for me! I can take a walk as far as the vineyards. But if the hunters danced at just any time, every day would be like every other day, and I should never have any vacation at all."

So the little prince tamed the fox. And when the hour of his departure drew near –

"Ah," said the fox. "I shall cry."

"It is your own fault," said the little prince. "I never wished you any sort of harm; but you wanted me to tame you ."

"Yes, that is so," said the fox.

"Then it has done you no good at all!"

"It has done me good," said the fox, "because of the color of the wheat fields." And then he added:

"Go and look again at the roses. You will understand now that yours is unique in all the world. Then come back to say goodbye to me, and I will make you a present of a secret."

The little prince went away, to look again at the roses.

"You are not at all like my rose," he said. "As yet you are nothing. No one has tamed you, and you have tamed no one. You are like my fox when I first knew him. He was only a fox like a hundred thousand other foxes. But I have made him my friend, and now he is unique in all the world."

And the roses were very much embarrassed.

"You are beautiful, but you are empty," he went on. "One could not die for you. To be sure, an ordinary passerby would think that my rose looked just like you – the rose that belongs to me. But in herself alone she is more important than all the hundreds of you other roses; because it is she that I have watered; because it is she that I have put under the glass globe; because it is she that I have sheltered behind the screen; because it is for her that I have killed caterpillars (except the two or three that we saved to become butterflies); because it is she that I have listened to, when she grumbled, or boasted, or even sometimes when she said nothing. Because she is 'my' rose."

And he went back to meet the fox.

"Goodbye," he said.

"Goodbye," said the fox. "And now here is my secret, a very simple secret: It is only with the heart that one can see rightly; what is essential is invisible to the eye."

"What is essential is invisible to the eye," the little prince repeated, so that he would be sure to remember.

"It is the time you have wasted for your rose that makes your rose so important."

"It is the time I have wasted for my rose," said the little prince, so that he would be sure to remember.

"Men have forgotten this truth," said the fox. "But you must not forget it. You become responsible, forever, for what you have tamed. You are responsible for your rose."

"I am responsible for my rose," the little prince repeated, so that he would be sure to remember.

For precious moments, the crowd remained completely silent. With one common heart, the people of Point Loma said goodbye to their friend, the crazy guy on the bench. As teary eyed Point Lomans said farewell to Mayor Jeff Pastorino, I wondered if he would have cared that his life of isolation would have touched so many people. That is another question without an answer, but I know I cared. And I know that a lot of others cared. A most unlikely man led us into ourselves and helped us touch the face of our own humanity.

Father Joe Carroll addresses the crowd as Chris Pastorino stands by his side

Chapter Seventeen
Behind the Mask

If you believe the stories told by the people of Point Loma, Jeffrey Q. Pastorino was a successful business man who fell off the deep end. He was also an attorney broken by the stresses of the world. He was a CPA who walked away from his practice, his family and his career. He was a boat yard worker, a writer, a college educated researcher, an economist and an employee of the government.

People wondered and speculated over the years he sat on the bench. He was none of these things. In many respects, the true story of Jeffrey Pastorino was far too common to have ever been believed by those of us that observed him over the years. His life reflected the difficulties faced by others suffering from schizophrenia and sitting on their benches around the world or walking the streets looking for themselves as they listen to the voices in their heads.

It was warm and muggy on Thursday July 11, 1957. The Philadelphia Phillies had taken the last three games from the Dodgers and Robin Roberts was getting ready to pitch the opening game of a series against the Cubs. Commuters listened to Elvis Presley singing *Let Me Be Your Teddy Bear* on their car radios as they drove to work. The space race between Russia and the United States was about to take off with the launch of Sputnik. Catherine Pastorino was in Abington Hospital, just outside of Philadelphia giving birth to her fifth and sixth sons, first Jeffery, then fifteen minutes later, his non-identical twin Christopher.

David, born in 1948, was the oldest. Michael arrived a year later. Peter and Jerry followed. Raising six boys in the 1950s was a big job for Catherine and Daniel Pastorino. Daniel was a first generation Italian American who learned the business of a shoemaker from his father. Guglielino and Francesca Pastorino were part of the wave of Italian immigrants to the United States around the dawn of the twentieth century. Guglielino opened a shoemaker shop in the heart of Philadelphia. They lived in a small house less than a mile from the shores of the Delaware River. Jeffrey's father, Daniel, was the youngest of Guglielino's and Francesca's five children.

Growing up in the Pastorino household was as normal as one could expect in a family of six boys separated by only nine years. Skinned knees and elbows, sibling rivalry, an occasional scrap, plenty of sports and outdoor activities. Both Jeff and Chris loved soccer and became fairly good at it. They went to a Catholic school where they spent their fair share of time getting into trouble with the nuns.

When Jeff was in the fourth grade, a fire in the family home forced the family to move to an apartment in the northern suburbs of Philadelphia. They moved a number of times in the

Even before their third birthday, Jeffrey (left) was the gregarious, outgoing twin while Chris (right) was the more serious, pensive brother.

ensuing years living in Oreland, Fox Chase, Roslyn and Southampton. The boys began attending public schools in the fifth grade. As a result of moving in the middle of the school year, the boys lost a grade and were the oldest members of their class. By the time they entered junior high school, they started drifting apart. Chris was more studious and into sports; Jeff earned respectable grades, but only as good as necessary. He was discovering his natural social abilities and was popular with fellow students. He also began to discover girls and had more than his share of girl friends.

In 1969 when Jeff was ready to enter junior high school, the war in Vietnam had reached its crescendo. More than 33,000 Americans had died in a war that had torn the country asunder. Michael Pastorino, Jeff's older brother was a Green Beret and one of more than a half million American troops in Vietnam by the end of April. President Nixon authorized secret peace talks in Paris in the hope of bringing the conflict to an end.

That November, Jeff's father received a phone call saying that Michael was missing. The following day, Jeff and Chris were at their father's shoe repair shop when two uniformed men walked through the door. "We regret to inform you . . . ", they began. Michael had been killed in action in Vietnam. The family was devastated, but Jeff and Chris took the news hard. Jeff seemed to somehow be permanently changed from that point forward.

Jeffrey (left) and Chris (right) watch as their father, Daniel, works in his shoe repair shop in 1969

The wages of a shoemaker didn't cover many luxuries in Philadelphia in the seventies, especially when trying to feed a family of growing boys. If the boys were to have any spending money, they would have to earn it themselves. Chris had a paper route. Jeff got a job at a small grocery store. Jeff enjoyed working and enjoyed getting paychecks even more. Customers loved him because of his magnetic personality. His strong work ethic made him a favorite of the store owner who took him under his wing and began training him in the art of a butcher.

Jeff enjoyed his work and with time became a valued employee and butcher. The store owner put increasing levels of trust in Jeff. By the time Jeff was sixteen, he would run the store in the owner's absence. With increasing responsibilities came higher pay. Jeff was frugal and managed his money well.

In the early seventies, America was a culture in turmoil. Vietnam was winding down, the Beatles, Rolling Stones and Bob Dylan led a revolution in the music world, cheap gas and muscle cars drove us to a social azimuth of luxury and excess. Bell bottoms and Nehru jackets were commonplace. Jeff accented his highly social lifestyle with flashy clothes meticulously decorating his thin, handsome, Latin persona. He was the envy of his peers when he paid cash for his 1972 Pontiac GTO with its 6.5 liter engine that gobbled up any other car on the road. The car seemed to reflect his personality; it was fast, powerful and attention getting bright orange.

By the time Jeff entered the eleventh grade, he had attained a financial standing equaled by few people ten years his senior. His social life was fabulous. He was popular and had money, a car and a girl on each arm. He could see no reason to stay in school. He dropped out mid way through the eleventh grade. Jeff went to work fulltime at the grocery store as the assistant manager. He was only seventeen years old.

He took his job seriously and continued to excel at it. In his off hours, he was a dapper social animal full of testosterone and thirsty for fun and adventure. His best friend, Chuck Long, moved into Jeff's apartment. Jeff and Chuck split the cost of a twenty-foot power boat and spent countless hours cruising the nearby Delaware River. The boat was portentously named "Miss Conduct". Life was good for Jeffrey Pastorino, but dark clouds were forming on the horizon.

The five Pastorino brothers at Chris' wedding in 1980.
Left to right: Peter, Chris, Jeffrey, Jerry and David

By the time Jeff was in his early twenties, he was making good money as a butcher, had a steady girlfriend named Mary and when he wasn't working, he was doing what other young adults were doing in the late seventies, partying. Together with his friends, he would have a few beers on the weekend. But deep within his mind, the demons of schizophrenia were stirring. His friends thought he was moody. His thoughts sometimes became a little more grandiose than reality proved justifiable.

His eccentric behavior strained his relationship with Mary. They had been together long enough that Jeff's brother, Chris assumed they would ultimately marry and settle down. Jeff was stunned when Mary broke off the relationship. He took it hard and his behavior became more erratic and unpredictable. Friends had no reason to assume schizophrenia was the cause of his increasingly strange conduct.

Jeff and his good friend, Chuck Long, together with their friends from the neighborhood socialized so much, they took to calling themselves "The Gorson Gang" after the name of the street on which they lived. When the cold grey of winter had outlasted its welcome in eastern Pennsylvania, Chuck and the others decided the warm, sandy beaches of Florida would be a welcome respite from the cold. Everyone was ready and willing except Jeff. Despite his love of the social high life, Jeff was dutifully bound to his job. He knew the owner of the Colonial Market depended heavily upon him to help run the store and didn't want to leave him in a bind. Jeff begged off.

Late one afternoon, Chuck's small motor home pulled up behind the market. The "gang" lured Jeff outside, put a bag over his head and used duct tape to bind his hands and feet. They threw him in the back of the van and drove straight to Florida to party for a week.

Jeff left with nothing more than the clothes on his back. He feared he'd lose his job, a fear that proved to be justified. The Gorson Gang partied for a week in Florida, but the party wasn't the fun they'd expected. The stress seemed to weigh heavily on Jeff's mind. Something seemed to snap. Chuck said that after the Florida trip, Jeff was never the same.

One night some time after the Florida trip, Jeff had been partying more than must have been appropriate. The police stopped him in his GTO and cited him for driving under the influence of alcohol. He spent the night in jail. Upon his release, he vowed to fight the charges in court. He believed that with the best legal representation available he would prevail. To the surprise of friends and family, he announced he would represent himself in front of a jury of his peers.

When the day of the trial arrived, Jeff showed up dressed to the nines doing his best imitation of a slick East Coast defense attorney. Unfortunately, that's where the resemblance ended. Jeff's first performance as a defense lawyer was memorable, but only in the way Custer's performance at the Little Big Horn was memorable. Jeff was sentenced to spend some time behind bars.

While incarcerated, Jeff's behavior worsened. He was taken to Norristown State Hospital for evaluation. When Norristown was first opened in 1879, it was the "State Lunatic Hospital at Norristown". By now, the demons in Jeff's mind had grown strong enough to warrant a six month stay in the hospital.

Norristown State Hospital c. 1930

The details of the diagnosis and treatment remain sealed, but it's safe to say Jeff's schizophrenia was now in full bloom. In the forties and fifties, shock therapy was used regularly at Norristown. There's no way to know if shock therapy was still in use when Jeff was there, but it is certainly possible. Something happened there that had a dramatic impact on Jeff. It appears he never drank alcohol again throughout the remainder of his life.

Drugs were definitely used to treat patients at Norristown. They were used to mitigate the effects of schizophrenia. When Jeff was finally released, he was undoubtedly being treated chemically for his mental illness, probably with Thorazine.

By the time Jeff left Norristown, he'd lost his apartment, his job and more. Chuck Long had married, had two young children and was living in the home of his mother. To help his friend, the Longs opened their doors to Jeff and he moved in.

When Jeff took his medication he was one person; when he didn't, he was another. When he was medicated, he was calmer, more subdued. He wasn't the dynamic social animal he had grown to be. He didn't like it. He was also embarrassed by his condition and the fact that he was dependent upon his meds.

Jeff also faced a dilemma that many schizophrenics must confront. Under medication, he felt sufficiently "normal" that he had trouble convincing himself he needed to take the pills. He was "cured". When he felt that way, it was too easy to skip a pill or two or more. Without the pill, the demons returned with a vengeance.

The living arrangements weren't conducive to complete harmony. A young married couple with two toddlers living under the roof of the matriarch can be difficult enough. Throw a young male schizophrenic into the mix and it becomes only a matter of time before that bus goes over the cliff. And it did.

Recriminations, bizarre behavior and delusions were piled onto the already flammable mixture of circumstances. The members of the Long family were stunned by Jeff's strange conduct. At one point, Jeff insisted that he, not Chuck, was the genetic father of Chuck's two young children. Jeff said there had been a mix up at the hospital. The Longs found an increasingly pressing need for Jeff to find other living arrangements and Jeff continued to fight a losing battle with his demons.

One November evening in 1982, Jeff erupted and announced he was moving to Paris. The next morning, he was gone. No one in the Long household knew where Jeff had gone. They knew only relief.

Jerry Pastorino, Jeff's older brother, lived in Florida. Jeff showed up at Jerry's house in need of a place to stay. Jerry and his wife reluctantly let Jeff move in with them. Jeff got a job at a local grocery store and returned to his life as a butcher. To the casual onlooker, Jeff was leading a fairly normal life going to work every day and coming home every night. But the truth was Jeff was desperately holding on to life with both hands. He was constantly at war with his mind and he wasn't winning. After about six months, both Jerry and his wife rose from bed, dressed and left for work. When they returned, Jeff was gone. They never saw him alive again.

The next few years are in part a mystery. Jeff may have been committed for additional treatment for his schizophrenia, but with only partial success. He ran from his demons not realizing they would be going with him. He went north to Toronto, Canada. His behavior was too off the charts to fit in without notice and was taken into custody by the authorities. He was allowed to leave the country.

It wasn't long before Jeff appeared in California. His delusions ran wild. He apparently had one or two run-ins with the law while in California. Once, he was arrested for renting a car and "forgetting" to return it. Another time, he was arrested for brandishing a gun when he was involved in a dispute. It turned out to be a toy gun, but the authorities felt it was serious enough to arrest him nonetheless. It quickly became apparent Jeff had mental problems and he was placed in a mental health facility for evaluation and treatment. With medication, Jeff was moved into the Beverlywood Care Center, a sort of halfway house for mentally disturbed patients. He was unemployable.

In 2010, Beverlywood continues to serve the needs of California's mentally ill

With his mental illness now out of control, he was declared "mentally disabled" and began receiving monthly disability checks from the Social Security Administration.

Even with the assistance of his medications, Jeff experienced delusions of grandeur claiming to be a powerful official for foreign governments, an important international business entrepreneur and a high ranking military officer.

Jeff's demons were always with him encouraging him to live in an imaginary world that only he could see. He was frustrated by the present and haunted by his past. He remembered the embarrassments from the past, but his mental state left him unable to deal with them the way most people would. The follies of his past were rewritten in his mind as transgressions upon his honor and character.

It is hard enough to imagine the inner workings of the mind of a schizophrenic, let alone describe them. One of the most telling glimpses comes from a letter composed by Jeff in 1987. By this time, he was receiving his monthly checks from the government and was living in a

In 1987, Jeffrey tried to make it on his own and lived in this building in the heart of Hollywood, California

colorful section of Hollywood, California. His room was twelve feet square. It had a small sink, a shower, a bed and one window. In his more lucid moments, guilt and embarrassment weighed upon him more than he could bear. He continued to be tormented by memories of the time he spent living with the Long family. In a carefully typed letter to Rosemarie Long, the mother of his former best friend, he made his case. As would become his trademark on nearly everything he wrote the rest of his life, the letter was sent under the banner of a heady sounding entity. What follows is the text of the letter exactly as it was written.

FOREIGN EXCHANGE OF DEVELOPMENT

> *JEFFREY QUERINO PASTORINO*
> *1759 NORTH ORCHID AVENUE*
> *STUDIO #307-B*
> *HOLLYWOOD, CALIFORNIA 90028*
> *NOVEMBER 7, 1987*

MS. ROSEMARY LONG
1031 GORSON DRIVE   (CONFIDENTIAL)
WARMINSTER, PENNSYLVANIA. 18974

DEAR MS. LONG:

In regard with my last visit at your home in November, 1982; To make things more simplified. I had made a full Genealogy Family Investigation. And Had found that Tommie, and Michelle were my children. And not Charles V. Long Jr. children. In the interested of avoiding a argument to this Geneology Family Investigation. Without any contradicted to my report. That Tommie, and Michelle mother had problems at Hospital of not knowing who father was! Her name that she using is Diane Xibos. She is not a American, but she is a Canadian. She was a friend of Charles wife! To the ridiculous of this realistic problem. That Charles V. Long Jr. had wrong children from Hospital! And Diane had another child of name of Douglus. In which you may had encounter him?

In preceded this formally to a persuaded. That my children are very mix-up! I had seen Tommie in California, and he is not sure about anything! Everything is mind of the matter! I had made Inquested in Bucks County Court System, in Pennsylvania. A problem with my children are assuming the certain of more children with another woman. That Jimmy McDonald also had encounter a problem at Hosiptal with wrong baby in Virginia. His wife is a brother that is Rickey Schorden, and a sister that is Heather. In which I had met Heather at work in Huntington Valley Prime Meats in Philadelphila. The lady at work was friend of Paul McDonald. I had recognize this problem of inhabitant children. I was not sure at time, but had strong feeling about children. I could say that I was sure, but did not know how to make a accepting indicated to this family problem.

Before I had visit Paris, France. I was sure that Tommie, and Michelle were my children. And had lelf for reason of hesitated of killing you all! I was very mad, to miss the important years of my children. It took a very, long time to make Legal System to a understanding. That a Family Genealogy Investigation was subsitted in propected to make things right. I am not a very like person, to the another Family Genalogy Investigation I had made were in good faith! With poor communication with Court System, in ordeal of what is a Family Genealogy Investigation! In the due respect of my descent in a birth of emulation to a contemplation to The Federal Crown of Canada! I was born in Toronto, Ontario. Canada. I was shipped to United States of heart problem. After I was born I had encounter a heart murmur. That was cause by my mother, and father. They had kept me up when I was sleeping, and did not get rested that I need.

My mother, and father names are Joan Rivers, and Jeff Corey. My father is a half-brother of Robert Redford, and he had star in move call Butch Casidy And Sundance Kid (1969). I had met your mother, and father! You mother that comes to house is your grandmother. I had met your mother at Norristown State Hosiptal. She was intake person at Hosiptal, on day of April 10, 1985; And met your father at Bucks County Correctional Centre, Doylestown, Pennsylvania. And had met some of your children there too! They had work there in Bucks County Correctional Centre in year of 1985; And also met your younger brother in Canada. At Toronto West Detention Centre. And met Charles V. Long Jr. Mother at Canada Immigration Centre. She is a Adjudicator for Canadian Government. And it had been confronted to me of a problem. In a increased studies by Foreign Exchange of Development. To a negative family of society. In most studies all family are in a similarity of being same! With perception of half-brothers and half-sisters in their Families. With haved children with other people.

In a consideration that Charles V. Long Jr. is subjected by his grandmother. Rosemary! Charles is your grandson! And your son has lots of children with different people. I think you discourage him and he is always in troubled. The frist initiative you should make is contact his father. People with mental problems haved problem with people they a refused by. And is not always real father, or mother, but they are told that! I had met some of Charles brothers in Canada, in family side of his mother. His mother, and father haved children with different people. And problem is not going to get better. They needed to get together with one another. I haved same problem with my own mother, and father. They haved children with different people. I haved over thirty half-brother with my family side of my father. With interested of a better understanding that I am very busy. I am starting a new government agency call "Foreign Exchange of Devlopment. And another new agency call "Orbit Space of Development".

I don't have the time for old friends. In fact I do not have a friend! Most people I had met are family members. Charles, is a family member of a consin to my father side of family. I am not talking to my father side of family! They owe me child support in non-support to me. I had met another one of your sons in California. At Bevenlywood Broad and Care in Los Angeles. He is in big trouble too! And had met Charles V. Long Sr. father at Veterans Hospital in West Los Angeles. He is a fraud, and he has another sons in California. I do feel that Charles has no time to get together with me. He has his family to see! And I have a business to get together. I would like to ask you for a favorite. If you could call my last employer, and have him sented me my last week pay check. I had written to him about this. And he dos'nt sented me my requested.

If there is any money from boat sale. Please sented to my address above this letter. I had moved to Hollywood, California. I had a few problems with circumisions! I had encounter secretmylers, about ten of them. In my past life I had got very ill from these circuision. I am a double five star General! I had found that I would of not haved any children with two girlfriends that I had. Their family is not my kind of people! I will refused to talk to them! I will only see my own children, and I do not have to see them! I will refused to see them, or talk to them. In fact I do not talk to anybody that don't write. People forget what they say! I would like everything in writing!

P.S. If you have time! Make a collected call to Tommie! And tell him he is full of shit! I am his real father! And he has a lot of growing up to do! "Thank you!

Best Regards

JEFFREY QUERINO PASTORINO
FEDERAL CROWN OF CANADA *****
FOREIGN AGENT, PRESIDENT

Jeff had put up a noble fight, but had clearly lost the war. His demons ruled and would rule the rest of his life.

Jeff struggled to survive in the Los Angeles area passing through moments of lucidity like a man on a swing. To the lay person, it is almost unfathomable how Jeff could have had such a singularity of purpose in his quest to build a business or "governmental" organization while spending so much of his time in a fantasy world. It would occupy much of his time in the ensuing twenty-two years.

For the next three or four years, Jeff spent his time dreaming of a grand future while living in the Los Angeles area. Try as he might, the dreams were always elusive. He would write letters to government officials, business people and others. Sadly, the plans and proposals of a hebephrenic schizophrenic started on point, but quickly meandered into seemingly bizarre and illogical diatribes. His repeated failures to generate support for his ideas didn't deter him from trying.

The old flashy dressing Jeff Pastorino knew that clothes could make the man. To rebuild his image and establish his credibility in the business world, Jeff invested in a smart and stylish business suit. By

1992, he concluded his Hollywood neighborhood didn't have the progressive, forward thinking entrepreneurs he needed for his success. Dressed to the nines and ready to finally ascend to his rightful place as a business leader, he went to where he'd heard the well healed segment of society lived in mansions and kept their yachts. He walked away from Hollywood with nothing but the clothes on his back, dapper as they may have been, and set out for Point Loma, California. He carried hope in his heart, his dreams and fantasies in his mind.

Jeff became a prisoner in his own mind. He sat in Point Loma for eighteen years conjuring up grandiose ideas and plans, but they never went far beyond his bench. It seemed there was nowhere he could go to bring them to fruition so that's exactly where he went, nowhere. With time, he sank deeper and deeper into his own world. By 1999, the Social Security Administration had heard nothing from or about him in years. They sent him a letter saying that in the absence of medical evidence to the contrary, they would be forced to assume he had been "cured" and he would no longer receive his monthly checks. Jeff was no more capable of presenting his case to the agency than he was getting a job. When he read the letter, he did the only thing he could at the time – nothing. His benefits stopped. But by this time, the community had begun the process of adopting Jeff. He didn't need much. All his worldly possessions were in the duffel bag someone had given him. He had a light weight sleeping bag for the evenings and a bench during the day.

When he arrived in Point Loma, Jeff sat down on a bench. He dreamed. He planned. He wrote letters to the White House and the Department of the Treasury. His ideas were creative to say the least. After he died, the last of his business plans were in his duffel bag. Each one was carefully hand written on a piece of paper with his company's name at the top, "INVESTMENT GROUP BANKER, INC."

One plan involved what Jeff named "HAUTE SPA". It was to be an "educational salon hair treatment for oil, hair." Once cut, the hair would be used to collect the oil and do something further with it. We'll never know the rest of the details. It was the only unfinished plan that The Mayor left behind when he died.

Jeff came to Point Loma in the early nineties. He sat down. He carried with him his dreams, his hopes and his fears. He hid from his demons by sitting in one spot for all those years. He was safe there and he knew that if he tried to leave, the demons would follow him wherever he went.

Chapter Eighteen
Looking Back

Every day, thousands of people turned their heads as they drove by Jeffrey Pastorino. Some never noticed him sitting on his bench. That's the way he liked it. Thousands of others saw him and never gave him a second thought. Some wondered who he was and why he sat in the same place every day of the year. Histories were created in the ether about this homeless man. The stories constructed by the strangers that saw him were no more rooted in reality than were Jeff's own thoughts and the world in which he lived.

A few people penetrated his world for fleeting instants. Fewer yet were fortunate to get to know him well enough to see him for what he was – a real, frail, sensitive, caring human being. He didn't choose to live his life as a schizophrenic.

Given his mental illness, he was destined to a life where he faced an endless series of rejections. He did his best, just like we all do, but ultimately he dealt with life in the only way he could. He secreted himself away from the world. He withdrew. He chatted with his demons. He listened to his thoughts and elected not to share them with others; he knew you wouldn't understand.

In my years as a writer and reporter, I've met many famous and influential people, Presidents, senators, Nobel Prize winners, movie stars, Hall-of-Fame athletes, and a host of others. But few people have had a greater impact on me than Jeff Pastorino. The Mayor touched my life both directly and indirectly.

Like the little prince that befriended the fox, I look back on the joys that came from the years I knew Jeff. I remember his first wave like it happened this morning. I fondly recall the many times he thought about what we discussed and did a bit more work on the subject to help me understand, like the time he gave me a picture of a $100,000 bill. I treasure the memories of Jeff always showing his gratitude for the little things. Thanks to him, I now try to do more of the same. I feel special knowing that a person who wanted to be invisible invited me into his world for friendship and sharing. I feel fortunate in knowing that Jeff trusted me as his friend. His friendship was a rare and magnificent gift. For these small joys, I am grateful.

Jeffrey Pastorino also had a profound impact indirectly, not just on my life, but on the lives of countless others. It wasn't his intention. He was unaware of his role as a teacher.

Those who were open to his teaching learned, as I did, that life's less fortunate are human beings with the same feelings, emotions, desires, needs and frailties as the rest of us. If we turn our backs on them, we turn our backs on ourselves and on humanity.

Jeff dealt with things he couldn't control by simply not caring about them. A common folkism known as The Serenity Prayer says,

> *God, grant me the serenity*
> *To accept the things I cannot change,*
> *Courage to change the things I can,*
> *and wisdom to know the difference.*

Jeff took it to heart. He worried about little. When the twin towers collapsed in New York on that fateful September day in 2001, the nation was fraught with worry – not Jeff. "It doesn't affect me," he said. He was right.

The Mayor showed us that we should never give up our dreams. Even though his designs and plans proved to be of little or no value in the business world, those same dreams sustained Jeff from day-to-day. Jeff never stopped dreaming and his dreams gave him hope for a better day with each sunrise.

The light didn't shine on the Mayor's greatest lessons until he was gone. It was then people came out from their enclaves in Point Loma to say they regretted not offering to help him more often. As neighbors stood by his bench with tears running down their cheeks, they realized that life is too short to wait to reach out. Opportunities passed are opportunities lost. Jeff showed that putting aside petty differences and reaching out to family and friends can't wait until tomorrow. Tomorrow may never come. Our chances to do good things, to love, to care and to contribute to humanity are not without end.

Jeff also made us all take a step back and think about what it means to be a part of the human race. He had nothing in common with any of us, but he proved he was just like all of us. At a time when the world is in turmoil, the nation struggling to remain whole and Americans building and retreating behind their artificial fortresses, Jeff reminded us of our humanity. People came together over this homeless man in a way that would have been impossible in any other circumstance. The rich, the poor, the old and young, immigrants, people from many countries and cultures all came together around Jeff. They were united briefly with the knowledge that deep within all of us there is a common thread of goodness. It is too easy to forget that human beings are programmed to be loving, caring creatures. We're programmed to help one another. We have an innate sense that tells us that only by caring about each other can we realistically expect to be cared about.

I still walk every morning with Liz. To this day, when we walk by the bench we look for the Mayor. His spirit still sits there reminding me that when I see one of society's downtrodden, there is some goodness within. When I see someone acting foolishly or aggressively, I know a caring human being is hiding somewhere behind the mask. When I see someone just trying to hold on to life with fear and urgency in his eyes, that person is little different than any of us.

When Jeff Pastorino died, people from all walks of life came together over him. He proved to be our "everyman". With each rising sun, we saw ourselves sitting on his bench, maybe only a half step away from crazy. And maybe only a half step away from caring. Jeff said, "Don't let it be too late."

There was a slight mist coming in off the ocean this morning when we walked. As I passed the bench, I remembered how the Mayor never forgot to say, "Hey, thanks" for every small kindness. I thought I'd better return the favor and say thanks to him. Maybe I'll write a book.

A block past his office, I stopped and turned toward the bench. The sun was breaking through the morning mist and brightening his office. I watched as an unshaven, road weary stranger put his backpack on the Mayor's bench and sat down to rest.

The weather in Point Loma, California is close to perfect today. I know this because the weather in Point Loma is close to perfect every day.

A plaque on the bench commemorates "The Man on the Bench"

About the Author

h. Alton Jones is a native of Detroit, Michigan. He is an honors graduate of Michigan State University where he attended undergraduate and graduate school in chemical engineering. He studied for his Ph.D. at the University of Arizona in Tucson. He began his writing and reporting career in Ann Arbor, Michigan in 1966 and worked in the broadcast industry in Detroit, Denver, Miami and Portland, Oregon. After leaving the news business to found and run a successful software company, he returned to the media world in 2000 writing a regular column in an Arizona newspaper for nearly ten years. Together with his wife of more than twenty-five years, Liz McCarty, he still travels the world seeking adventure and new horizons. When not travelling, he splits his time between homes in San Diego, California and Scottsdale, Arizona.

www.54Candles.org